CHILDREN OF POVERTY
WITH HANDICAPPING CONDITIONS

CHILDREN OF POVERTY
WITH HANDICAPPING CONDITIONS
How Teachers Can Cope Humanistically

By

NANCY POWELL DIXON, Ed.D.

Department of Human Services
Western Carolina University
Cullowhee, North Carolina

CHARLES C THOMAS • PUBLISHER
Springfield • *Illinois* • *U.S.A.*

83-674

Published and Distributed Throughout the World by
CHARLES C THOMAS • PUBLISHER
Bannerstone House
301-327 East Lawrence Avenue, Springfield, Illinois, U.S.A.

© *1981, by* CHARLES C THOMAS • PUBLISHER

ISBN 0-398-04478-3

Library of Congress Catalog Card Number: 80-28296

*With THOMAS BOOKS careful attention is given to all details of
manufacturing and design. It is the Publisher's desire to present books that are
satisfactory as to their physical qualities and artistic possibilities and
appropriate for their particular use. THOMAS BOOKS will be true to those
laws of quality that assure a good name and good will.*

Library of Congress Cataloging in Publication Data

Dixon, Nancy Powell.
    Children of poverty with handicapping conditions.

    Bibliography: p.

    Includes index.
    1. Socially handicapped children — Education — United States.   2. Handicapped
children — Education — United States.   I. Title.
LC4091.D58   371.9   80-28296
ISBN 0-398-04478-3

Printed in the United States of America
PS-RX-1

PREFACE

Students entering the teaching profession face many difficult but exciting and challenging problems. Not only must teachers deal with large numbers of students, they must interact with those from varying home backgrounds and cultures. Since the passage of Public Law 94-142, all teachers must also expect to encounter students with varying degrees of physical, mental, and emotional handicaps. These backgrounds and conditions do not coincide with most teachers' past experiences and cultures. The majority come from the white, middle-class stratum of our society. In talking with college students who have completed their student teaching this author so frequently has heard "I didn't know children like that existed," or "I wasn't prepared for the shock of the intensity of their problems."

In the past, handicapped children of poverty have been virtually ignored as a group. They deserve the immediate attention of educators. These youngsters are found in our schools in both special education classes and in regular classes. All teachers should be prepared to deal with the problems associated with poverty as well as handicapping conditions.

Education students should be made aware of the existence of such children in our schools early in the undergraduate teacher preparation programs. In addition, the college programs have a responsibility to provide knowledge about poverty and handicaps. They need to furnish guidelines that teachers may use in order to cope successfully with the difficult home and school situations.

School systems may supply assistance to teachers through workshops and in-service training programs. The better prepared teachers are to handle effectively the problems that children of poverty with handicapping conditions bring to the classroom, the better off society will be when these youngsters are functioning as independent, contributing citizens. Our educational system should strive to have a positive effect on the lives of these children.

v

This book presents case studies that describe children of poverty with handicaps in the school, the home, and hospital settings. Some of the descriptions are bleak and shocking. A few are left open-ended and unresolved, but they represent realistic situations that teachers are likely to encounter during their careers. The vignettes may be used in courses or workshops as a basis for role-playing activities or as groundwork for examining the various disabilities one may find in children who are receiving special education. It is further suggested that the cases be presented a few at a time rather than as an entity. By so doing, the youngsters who are discussed will not lose their individuality.

Supplementary to each vignette are a number of stimulus questions. The instructor may use these questions to encourage discussions among students. They provide an opportunity for students to apply knowledge they have gained in course work and to voice their feelings and opinions through individual and group study. This author has successfully used these case studies in both graduate and undergraduate courses and in workshops. The purpose is to illustrate and emphasize the plight of children of poverty with handicapping conditions along with presenting humanistic approaches to dealing with the situations.

The Introduction defines the population of interest, sets a rationale for the book, and provides a discussion of humanistic approaches which may be used in working with youngsters who come from different cultural backgrounds and who have handicaps.

The case studies are composites of actual students that this author taught during her public school experience. The names, dates, and places have been changed in order to protect those involved.

It is to be noted that many of the teachers represented in the vignettes are young or new to the teaching profession. They have been used because this book has been written primarily for beginning teachers entering the field. Also, this author experienced contact with these children as a young, neophyte teacher.

There are other advantages to viewing children from this standpoint. First and second year teachers tend to be more objective about situations which they encounter. They are less likely to be influenced by community opinion or family histories of the children. As a result, they are able to form opinions from direct contact with the youngsters rather than from second and third hand reports in local gossip. This is not to say that beginning teachers have feelings and insights that become lost through the years, but rather that they are more nearly free from exposure to extraneous inputs that tend to color the relationships of even the best of teachers with their students.

Through this book it is hoped that college students will gain insights into the lives of many of the youngsters they will be teaching. The humanistic approaches presented may prove beneficial as a means of dealing with children who have such difficult problems.

This author wishes to express a deep appreciation to those inspiring teachers who made a difference in her life. Myrtle Davis and Frances A. Scott contributed knowledge and insight through the use of vignettes as a teaching tool. Mary M. Wood of the Program for Exceptional Children at the University of Georgia encouraged the production of this book.

Colleagues, former students, and friends who made meaningful contributions are Sandy Moore, Eunice Avriett, Betsy Williams, Sonia Mason, Helen Smith, Michelle Farina, Jane Schulz, Gurney Chambers, Betty Siegel, Tom Warren, Georgia Hickes, Brenda Anders, Annie Mac Eachirn, Patsy Warren, Dixie Cochran, Freddy Jones, and the students at Western Carolina University who responded in such helpful ways to the vignettes.

This book is dedicated to Jack and Myra Powell and George, Pete, and Susan Dixon.

Nancy Powell Dixon

CONTENTS

CHILDREN OF POVERTY
WITH HANDICAPPING CONDITIONS

INTRODUCTION

After leaving their colleges and universities, teachers in both special education and regular education are frequently confronted with perplexing problems in the classroom. The most disturbing situations often center around those youngsters who are handicapped, who come from poverty stricken families or, in many cases, are children with the combined limitations of both poverty and mental and physical handicaps. College students need to have exposure to such children and their environments before entering the classrooms as teachers. Knowledge about such situations may help to prevent what is commonly called "culture shock" or possibly even the loss of a potentially good teacher who simply was not prepared to deal with the problems these youngsters exhibit.

Faced with a child who has unpleasant body odor, what is the appropriate response of the teacher? Does the teacher provide showers at school, send a note home to the parents suggesting that Johnny be given a bath or, on a stronger note, that Johnny should not come back to school until he has bathed? Given a child with a physical deformity, should the teacher attempt to acquaint the family with possible medical assistance, or perhaps go so far as to place the family in contact with a physician? Where does the role of a teacher pass over to the role of teacher as social worker?

The teacher's attention should be directed toward those factors that affect classroom performance, but these, in many cases, cannot be divorced from the larger context of the pupil's relation to his family, to his peer group, and, most importantly, to his own self-image and self-worth.

The case studies presented in this book provide a realistic preview of some of the children and problems teachers are likely to encounter during their teaching careers. There is no single set of solutions that will work in every case, but by examining some of the humanistic goals, alternatives for coping with such situations are established.

Each vignette includes thought questions that not only call for an examination of the facts, but may stimulate alternative solutions and reactions. The value system of each reader will be an influential factor in how the questions are perceived and answered. Individual assessment as well as group discussions about the selections are suggested as a means of using the studies to their best advantage. It must be emphasized that often there are no right or wrong answers to the questions. The reader must feel comfortable about his solutions to the problems. For example, not all teachers would be willing to take student's clothes home to wash them, nor would they be willing to provide breakfast for youngsters. In many cases, these may not always be appropriate responses to the dirty or hungry child. The teacher who does not see such actions as the proper way to handle a situation is not any less humanistic or caring than one who does. It simply means that teachers, too, are different and need to approach problems in varying ways and degrees.

THE PROBLEMS

There exists in our wealthy and affluent country 7 million school age children who come from families with a yearly income of less than $6,200. According to the 1977 government guidelines, this figure and below is the qualifying poverty level for a family of four or more. These are the people who cannot afford to purchase adequate food, clothing, or shelter. They live with physical discomforts and the lack of security. A portion of these poverty stricken youngsters have the additional burdens of physical, mental, or emotional handicaps. They are the primary focus of this book.

In the 1960s there was an upsurge of interest in the education of children from low-income homes. This came about because of the recognition of a strong link between poverty and low school achievement. Thus, compensatory educational programs for these children were established. Almost twenty years later it is noted that children of poverty are no better off now than they were before the explosion of public and professional concern. This is reflected in the fact that the drop-out rate among these children is as high as 50 percent, and the number of people on welfare is climbing at a steady rate. Illiteracy among youngsters from families with incomes less than $3,000 per year is three times the national average (Vogt, 1973). Although many of the compensatory programs have failed, they are still supported as one of the major means of attempting to prevent disadvantaged children from falling behind academically.

A large majority of children being served in special education classes fall into this realm of poverty. This relationship is due in part to such factors as poor maternal nutrition, malnutrition, inadequate housing, and a greater exposure to hazards such as infections, diseases, and toxic substances. In addition, the home environments often do not provide the readiness background for learning that is crucial for a successful school experience.

With the passage of Public Law 94-142 both handicapped children of poverty, along with handicapped children from higher income homes, will benefit educationally. Youngsters with handicaps are defined as those who are "mentally retarded, hard of hearing, deaf, speech impaired, visually handicapped, seriously emotionally disturbed, orthopedically impaired, or other health impaired children, or children with specific learning disabilities."

These handicapped children differ in significant ways from their more normal counterparts. Their disabilities range in severity from mild to severe. The problems may encompass a range of handicaps or there may be only one limitation. Whatever the cause, degree, or scope of the handicap, through the new law, these youngsters will receive a free, appropriate education in the least restrictive environment. The child of poverty with no disability will not directly benefit from this law, but it is hoped that eventually, all children will profit from its passage.

The law requires that individual educational plans be written for each handicapped child. These plans include both long-term and short-term educational goals. This is necessary if an appropriate education is to be provided. On the other hand, there is another essential element in the learning process that is not attended to in the law. This is in the realm of affective teaching.

Humanistic theories of teaching attempt to provide this vital component. The definition of humanistic education explains this concept quite well. Combs (1978), along with other humanistic educators, has presented the following definition: "Humanistic Education is a commitment to education and practice in which all facets of the teaching-learning process give major emphasis to the freedom, value, worth, dignity, and integrity of persons."

Humanistic education provides an excellent framework for providing teachers with assistance in the affective sector of education. Teachers frequently leave colleges and universities ill-prepared to meet the challenges that are brought forth by the students with multiple problems of handicapping conditions and poverty. Teachers may have learned about the etiology, diagnosis, and prognosis of handicapping conditions along with strategies for remediating learning deficiencies, but nowhere in the coursework will one find solutions for coping with situations such as hunger, filth, neglect, and prostitution among youngsters they may encounter. While it is true that there is no one method that will solve all of the problems, humanistic education offers the best opportunity for providing such answers.

INFLUENCE OF PREJUDICE

There is much to be done if handicapped children of poverty are to have an opportunity to reach their full potential. Allport's (1954) model of prejudice may be used as an observational technique to identify the negative feelings of our society toward handicapped or culturally different people. An examination of current practices towards handicapped children and adults demonstrates the need for a change of attitude among the public, including school personnel.

The most subtle level of prejudice is speaking out against certain groups, for instance, telling "little moron" and ethnic-type jokes, or stating cultural generalities such as, "All Irish are drunks," "All Indians are lazy," or "All blacks smell bad."

The second level Allport identifies is avoidance. Many public schools have quite successfully hidden handicapped children away from the sight of the normal students by assigning them rooms in basements, trailers, unused buildings behind the school, etc.

The next level is that of clear-cut discrimination. Over the years adults have had jobs denied to them because of handicapping conditions, even when they were perfectly capable of handling the work. Even with the passage of new anti-discrimination laws, loopholes are found to continue the practice of job discrimination against many minority groups.

Healthy people have set up physical barriers that work to prevent the physically handicapped from enjoying the same pleasures and benefits as themselves. In the past, handicapped people have been prevented from attending churches, schools, and even voting precincts, because of the absence of wheelchair ramps, doors wide enough to allow wheelchairs to enter, and elevators. Laws are changing to provide greater access to public buildings, but these barriers are still prevalent and are a major form of discrimination against physically disabled persons.

The fourth level of prejudice is physical attack. It was the observation of this author that in public schools it was more often the children from low-income families who received the largest portion of corporal punishment, not the youngsters from middle or upper-class families. Also, the students who were receiving special education tended to be used as examples for the rest of the school.

The last level is that of extermination. For over a quarter of a century sterilization on "misfits" was practiced to a large degree in many states. Mentally retarded and emotionally disturbed people were sterilized without their knowledge or consent. Sterilization was accepted as part of the eugenics movement and continues today in some states that still maintain antiquated laws in regard to this subject.

Prejudice toward people who are different definitely exists in our own society. Through new laws, strides are being made in overcoming many of the barriers, but until the public is given the opportunity to meet and learn about people with differences, these negative feelings will continue to propagate. It is hoped that by mainstreaming handicapped youngsters into regular classrooms and settings when possible, the normal students will have an opportunity to experience positive interactions with the disabled children to such an extent that the threat of prejudice will be lessened or even eradicated.

BASIC NEEDS

In order to understand further the people who are impoverished or who have handicapping conditions, it is helpful to examine first the basic needs of all people. Maslow (1954) has established what he believes to be a hierarchial arrangement of human values. At the lowest end of the continuum are the basic survival needs. This includes physiological needs such as air, water, food, sleep, elimination, etc. Safety needs follow. In order to function, people need to have a feeling of security and protection from harm. Social needs are received from the reaction of those surrounding us. Included here are feelings of belonging-ness, love, and self-esteem. Purkey (1978) states that if we are viewed as able, valuable, and responsible, then we will see ourselves in a similar light.

The last level of Maslow's hierarchy falls under psychological needs. Only when the previous needs are met is one able to function at this level. It includes the ability to learn, to appreciate aesthetic beauty, and to strive for self-actualization. Self-actuali-zation is defined as the ideal state of being or utilizing all potential to a maximum state. Carl Rogers (1962) sees this as a "fully functioning" person. This is one who is dynamic as opposed to static, is sensitive to the needs of the self and others, has a quality of immediacy, and is self-confident and productive. However, few people ever actually reach this highest plateau. One survey identifies such historical personalities as Abraham Lincoln, Eleanor Roosevelt, Albert Einstein, and Albert Schweitzer as being examples of fully functioning people.

Basically speaking, handicapped and impoverished people, too, are subject to the same needs as more normal people, and they also strive to become self-actualized. Anyone is capable of reaching this level, even those with physical and mental handi-caps. Adaptations may have to be made, but it is possible.

There are areas that require a stronger emphasis, and for those who intend to work with impoverished or handicapped people, it is helpful to examine those more pertinent factors. Weinstein and Fantini (1968) have identified what they consider to be the three most prevalent concerns of poverty-stricken people. The first of these is *self-rejection*, which reflects a basic need for a positive self-image. *Disconnectedness* from other members of society reflects a need to feel part of a group. The third concern is that of *powerlessness*. This reflects a need for the economically poor to gain a greater control over their lives.

The concerns of handicapped people are remarkably similar. It has been suggested that the self-concepts of disabled people are lower than the normal population. Because of a handicapping condition, many people feel that they do not belong, that they are isolates in a healthy world. These people are desperately seeking companionship and a sense of unity with their fellow beings. This sector of the population also feels a lack of power or control over their lives. Often this stems from a dependency upon others for either physical help or mental guidance. Whatever the reasons, poverty and handicapping conditions tend to produce individuals with three basic needs: identity, power, and connectedness. By keeping these in mind, teachers may use humanistic education to a more comprehensive degree.

POSITIVES AND NEGATIVES OF POVERTY IN THE CLASSROOM

The majority of teachers come from middle-class backgrounds. They tend to impose their values upon deprived students. Often the students are unable to accept or assimilate these values that so often conflict with their upbringing. When the student does try to adopt new and different values, the teacher may misinterpret or fail to recognize his efforts to achieve and meet the alien demands. In order to provide teachers with a knowledge base about the values of children from poverty stricken homes, an examination of both their weaknesses and strengths will be made.

According to Passow (1967) some general characteristics and deficiencies of children of poverty are as follows:

1. Often the child comes from a home which is traditional and somewhat religious.
2. He has established a "mind set" on beliefs about morality, punishment, education, the role of women and intellectuals, and customs.
3. He does not wish to adopt a middle-class way of living, but he does want to improve personal comforts.
4. He values masculine traits and views academics as unmasculine. He is often anti-intellectual.
5. He is often suggestible, but at the same time he is suspicious of new things.

6. He blames others for his failures.
7. He is frequently superstitious and ignorant about many things.
8. What people do is more important to him than what people think.
9. He is able to function with short-term rather than long-term goals in mind.

Limitations that may influence the classroom setting are as follows:

1. The child is often slow at cognitive tasks, but may be persistent when the content has meaning and value.
2. He learns in small steps from part to whole.
3. He thinks in concrete terms rather than abstractly.
4. He experiences difficulty when teaching styles are changed.
5. He has not learned how to be successful in school. He may know how to ask and answer questions. He does not seem to know how to study, and he does not know how to relate to the teacher.
6. He has difficulty in taking tests.
7. He is more interested in learning how to read, write and do arithmetic than participating in art, music, and social studies.

Being aware of these differences may assist teachers in leading the child into more successful learning experiences.

Reisman (1962) took a positive point of view in working with deprived youngsters. He felt that these students have much to offer society and that teachers can best help them to learn by taking their strengths into account rather than focusing on what they cannot do. Reisman, then identified what he termed the *overlooked positives* of impoverished children. These are presented as follows:

1. There is much cooperativeness among family members and less sibling rivalry.
2. The child of poverty enjoys being with other children more than the middle-class, individualistic, and self-oriented youngsters.
3. Teachers must prove themselves. The child is not influenced by status and prestige.
4. He is usually free of parental over-protection.

5. He accepts responsibility easily.
6. He does not feel guilty about his inadequacies.
7. He is interested in movement and action.
8. Frequently, he is superior in physical coordination and skills.
9. He learns visually rather than auditorily.

Of course, if children have the combined problems of poverty and handicapping conditions, these characteristics may not always hold true. Having an understanding of the differences, however, may provide teachers with an insight into the problems one is likely to encounter while working with these students.

A HIERARCHY FOR GROWTH

Many times, when teachers begin working with handicapped children, they have feelings about these students that are not positive. Teachers may be wrestling with fear or revulsion towards the children. Some may be overly dedicated and throw themselves into such a state of helping that they experience early "burn-out." Other teachers may have feelings of resentment for having to deal with handicapped students. Many good teachers feel frustrated. They want to do a proper job but are not equipped with the knowledge, experience, or assistance to go about this task successfully. These same feelings frequently occur when teachers are faced with children from low-income homes. A combination of these problems may lead to an unhappy experience for both the teachers and youngsters.

Higgs' (1975) study showed that attitudes may be changed as a result of advancing age, increase in the level of a person's information, or with related experiences. Thus, it stands to reason that teacher's negative feelings towards children of poverty with handicapping conditions may be changed in a more positive direction.

Basic to the success of any teacher are positive beliefs, feelings, and values that teachers hold in regard to themselves. They must have good self-concepts and high levels of self-understanding. Actions grow from the way one feels about oneself. Those who like themselves tend to like others, and those who reject themselves are likely to reject others. Thus, if a positive self-concept of the teacher is firmly established, there is a strong foundation for positive acceptance of children of poverty with handicaps (Combs, Avila, and Purkey, 1978).

A high level of self-esteem by the teacher is particularly critical in working with children who are different. Teachers of special children may be having difficulties adjusting to the demanding needs many of these youngsters have. A positive self-concept by the teacher may go a long way in assisting him or her to cope with these problems. This also lays the foundation for the teacher to be able to raise the self-concept of handicapped students.

The next step most teachers should experience is increasing their information about the cause and effect of handicapping conditions and poverty. Misconceptions concerning both areas exist in the minds of many professional people. For instance, they may think that cerebral palsy is contagious, that people who have handicapped children are being punished for previous misdeeds, or even that mentally retarded children are produced by "unnatural sex acts." Teachers may have the erroneous idea that children who use outdoor toilets carry germs and shouldn't be touched or that all poverty stricken people are lazy and don't want to work.

Gaining factual knowledge allows the teacher to view the child from a more realistic standpoint and thereby helps to eliminate the fear and revulsion that is common with the lack of facts and information. Through knowledge, attitudes may be modified, and, in many cases, this is imperative if teachers are to make an impact on the lives of the students they teach.

Another state that potential teachers of handicapped children of poverty should experience is that of contact or participation with the youngsters. Direct contact is the most widely agreed upon act in the literature for changing attitudes. This contact may be through short, structured, academic instructional periods, field trips to hospitals, special classes, or sheltered workshops. The greater the variety of experiences and the longer the duration of contact, the more effective the attitude change will be.

Acceptance is the fourth stage. Here, the teacher needs to feel that the student, no matter how severe his problem, is responsible, valuable, and able (Purkey, 1970). Rogers (1971, 1978) describes acceptance as a caring for the learner, but, at the same time, a nonpossessive caring. Acceptance is seeing the worth and value of each child. There is no room for pity, unrealistic hopes for a cure, or overindulgence. Children with special needs should be taught by teachers who accept them as they are, that is, children with the same feelings, desires, and hopes as normal youngsters.

The final element a successful teacher should develop is that of empathy. Empathy is having warmth, being sensitive to needs, or feeling with a child. Rogers (1971, 1978) has listed sensitivity as the first of his three necessary and sufficient conditions for effective helping relationships. The others are congruence and positive regard. Studies have shown that the most effective teachers are sensitive to the thinking, needs, feelings, and perceptions of their students.

It has been suggested here that there is a hierarchy of stages, or levels, through which teachers need to progress in order to be successful, particularily when the students are mentally or physically handicapped and come from poverty-level homes. These levels are a positive self-concept by the teacher, increase of factual knowledge about poverty and handicapping conditions, contact with handicapped persons, acceptance of the youngsters, and empathy with the children. Through university and college courses, workshops, and in-service programs, teachers may be provided with professional assistance to carry through the various stages discussed here. It is especially important that regular class teachers who will be having these children main-streamed into their classroom be provided with adequate preparation to cope with the problems.

HUMANISTIC APPROACHES

Many people believe that humanistic education is limited to being nice to children, but it is a more complicated process than this. Humanistic education focuses on the development of the child to his maximum human potential. The intent is to teach youngsters how to cope with the present and how to prepare themselves to deal with the future. Many disadvantaged handicapped students are unable to handle their present situations, much less prepare for what is to come. They are all capable of being functional and worthwhile adult members of our society and should be given the opportunity to do so. Unfortunately, the majority of educators operate in such a fashion that they are unable to assist the students to reach their highest potentials. Many teachers have the desire but not the knowledge to go about this task.

In the report included in the 1978 ASCD manual, *Humanistic Education: Objectives and Assessment,* the authors not only provided a definition of humanistic education, but they also presented the following seven basic goals that provides a framework to guide teachers in the skills of being humanistic.

The discussion that follows each goal is examined in relationship to an educational system that takes into account children of poverty with handicapping conditions. Activities and behaviors that teachers or administrators may use to develop a humanistic program for these students are presented.

1. **"Humanistic Education accepts the learner's needs and purposes and develops experiences and programs around the unique potentials of the learners."**

As discussed earlier, teachers who work with students who are obviously different from their more normal peer group must reach the level of complete and total acceptance of the child as he is. This acceptance may be especially difficult when the student comes from a vastly different socio-economic group, wears dirty clothes, or has an unattrative disfigurement. Teachers should not continuously try to change the student to fit middle-class standards and norms. Doing so may lead to frustration and anxiety on the part of both the teacher and student. Complete and total acceptance of the learner along with providing skills for coping in the student's environment is the focus of humanistic education.

Public law 94-142 requires that the uniqueness of the handicapped learner be taken into account. An Individualized Education Program (IEP) must be written for each child. These plans must be geared to the child's level, ability, and rate of learning. In other words, developmental characteristics and physical and mental abilities are considered more than age and grade. Both long-term goals and short-term objectives are specified. Teaching approaches in step by step patterns are presented along with alternative methods for reaching the desired goals. The learner is required to be involved in the writing of the IEP as much as possible. At the very least, the student must have the plans fully interpreted to him to her. One should be honest, realistic, and open with the child about his or her learning difficulties.

Teachers need to realize, however, that the IEPs are not totally encompassing. As the humanistic objectives point out, youngsters should be given the time and opportunity to learn more than what is stated in the IEP. Being allowed to think, to dream, to examine, to do free reading, etc., must be an integral part of the day's activities.

For those handicapped youngsters who are being mainstreamed into the regular classroom, it is vital that an open line of communication be established between the special class teacher and the regular class teacher. Both teachers need to sharpen their consultation skills. The academic work in these settings must be reinforcing. Assigning regular class work to be done during the special tutoring session is a waste of precious time, unless it has been prearranged and planned by both teachers. Also, students should never be penalized for being absent when they are in special class.

In developing programs teachers need to take advantage of any special talents and interests the youngster may have. These assets may be found in such areas as art, music, or physical education. The talents may be used creatively by the teacher to facilitate learning in the more academic-type subjects. The learner may be used as a resource. Asking him or her what works and what doesn't work can be a valuable tool in teaching. Through careful planning, teachers may work to develop the unique potential of their students, no matter how severe their handicaps or how low their economic level.

2. "'Humanistic Education' facilitates self-actualization and strives to develop in all persons a sense of personal adequacy."

In the earlier discussion of self-actualization, it was brought out that handicapped children of poverty can reach this level of development. In examining Rogers' definition of a fully functioning person one aspect is that there must be change or growth taking place in the person's life. Teachers are in a position to provide learning experiences that allow for the child continually to grow and develop. Teachers need to find the proper functioning levels of the child and proceed with his learning styles and interests in mind. Being sensitive to one's own needs and the needs of others should be an essential part of everyone's education. This may be taught through role-playing activities, games, and discussions of the individual differences and needs of each child. Canfield and Wells (1976), in their book, *100 Ways to Enchance Self Concept in the Classroom: A Handbook for Teachers and Parents,* provide excellent ways in which teachers may work to help improve the sensitivity of their students.

The quality of immediacy may be taught by stressing the importance of here and now, for example, we do our work today, because it needs to be done. Many children of poverty have difficulty seeing education as basic to meeting future needs, thus this attitude would easily be within their frame of reference.

Developing self-confidence in students is difficult, especially with handicapped youngsters. So often they have had such unsuccessful academic experiences that they are afraid of failure or feel that they are not capable. By building some degree of success into the everyday school program, it is possible to assist students to overcome at least part of their lack of self-confidence. This success should come through both the regular and special education classes.

Also, along these lines, peer-teaching is a valuable tool teachers may utilize. If the students are properly matched to personality and ability level, much learning may occur. It is helpful if the student who is doing the tutoring is one level higher than the one being tutored rather than several levels higher. In this manner, the youngster who is teaching will also profit from a review of the material he or she has just mastered. While it is true that handicapped students may not be able to do everything normal learners do, they may be led to discover talents and abilities they never knew existed within themselves.

Productivity is a vital aspect of our working society. With the proper guidance handicapped youngsters of poverty may find careers that will make use of their abilities. Thus, they may lead productive, useful lives. This guidance is especially critical in a student's prevocational and vocational training years. Teachers of this age group must familiarize themselves with the job opportunities that are available to and within the capabilities of students with varying handicaps within the community.

3. "Humanistic Education fosters acquisition of basic skills necessary for living in a multicultured society including academic, personal, interpersonal, communicative, and economic survival proficiencies."

Teachers and students alike need to acquaint themselves with the various cultures found in their region. For instance, in Florida, the schools are having to adjust to the large influx of Cuban children, and in the Southwest, the Chicano youngsters make up a substantial portion of the student body. Indian children are located in several parts of the country, including the South. This familiarization may be accomplished by unit projects, guest speakers, or having minority students share aspects of their culture with their classmates. Curriculum materials that exhibit multiethnic societies and varying family structures are of extreme importance.

Survival skills should be the main focus of any education program for handicapped children of poverty. This may be accomplished in the school mainstream or in special education classes. The educable youngsters must be taught to read vocabulary words, such as *men, women, danger, private, stop,* etc., all of which are necessary for coping in our society. In math, they must learn not only basic addition, subtraction, multiplication, and division, but, even more importantly, the concepts of time, money, and measurement. Trainable children need emphasis placed on learning self-help skills and language development.

An area of vital importance is that of communication. Teachers must work to develop communication skills in their students by providing such experiences as a sharing time each day, role-playing opportunities and a general stress on verbalizing ideas and feelings rather than the "shut-up, sit down, and do your work" philosophy that is so prevalent in our schools. A humanistic classroom should stress interpersonal relationships dealing with both the verbal and nonverbal actions of others. To assist teachers in becoming proficient in this area, administrators should encourage teachers to participate in workshops and in-service training programs with a focus on communication skills and human relations.

Physical proficiencies of each student may be examined through physical education classes. Children need to be taught bodily functions to the extent of not being ashamed or embarrassed of their bodies, even when a physical handicap is present. Sex education is essential for these youngsters and needs to be introduced along with social mores. If the youngster's family or culture takes a different viewpoint, one must approach this topic carefully, being careful not to put a negative connotation on the student's environment. Simply present the factual information and relate morals to societies expectations and pressures rather than an individual teacher's moral biases.

As stated earlier, prevocational and vocational options should be explored with the student. Home management techniques and community living are essential to a well-rounded development and lay the foundation for adult independence.

4. "Humanistic Education personalizes educational decisions and practices. To this end it includes students in the processes of their own education via democratic involvement in all levels of implementation."

In order for this goal to be carried out successfully with students, it is imperative that the democratic process be established early in a student's educational career. If it is not introduced until later, the chances of its being effective is minimized. It is difficult for older students to adjust to making choices and decisions freely. Curriculum decisions made early and jointly by the teacher and child will be more likely to have a lasting impact on the youngster's life.

The shared writing of the IEP for youngsters receiving special education is already an established procedure and certainly is a beginning for operating in a democratic fashion. Allowing free access of records to the student and his or her parents is another ingredient along these lines. Deciding on proper school placement is an area in which the student should be consulted. The psychological harm of having a child incorrectly placed in a special class or resource room may be worse than the actual handicap.

Other areas of student input may be in the selection of books, materials, films, topics for unit study, field trips, or any special activity in which they are expected to participate. The learner's likes and desires are important and student involvement is likely to result in greater understanding of basic concepts.

Assessment should be used as a way to plan future work. It provides information about the student's level of functioning and identifies his strengths and weaknesses. Teachers often misuse the evaluation process. Students should not be punished for their mistakes or errors in academic work, but rather be encouraged to try studying another way. If students are not grasping the concepts, teachers may need to discover other ways to present the material. Pointing out the positive aspects of students' work and utilizing their strengths is an efficient and humanistic method of using evaluation.

It is also advisable for teachers to be in tune with the personal aspect of their students' lives. They should be sensitive enough to detect signs of personal problems and know how to respond appropriately to the needs. At the very least, teachers should know who and what services are available to assist the youngsters. Being familiar with referral services in a community is a necessity, especially for special education teachers.

5. "Humanistic Education recognizes the primacy of human feelings and utilizes personal values and perceptions as integral factors in educational processes."

At the start of each school year, teachers need to establish a strong link between the school and home. One way to accomplish this is by home visits. Teachers not only can see the environments in which the children are living, but the personal contact with the parents on their own territory may also prove valuable if and when problems arise. This contact may aid teachers in seeing difficulties from the student's point of view. Home visits should be an integral part of every teacher's method of educating youngsters.

In addition to academic instruction, teachers should notice whether or not youngster's basic needs are being met. Even if teachers are unwilling or unable to provide breakfast for students who come to school hungry, seeking a solution through the principal or service organizations would allow the teacher to play a crucial role in this matter. Children simply cannot learn when they come to school cold, tired, and hungry.

It is hoped that a climate will be established in each classroom that allows for a variety of emotions among its students. If children must suppress their feelings and show a "stiff upper lip" or are not allowed to laugh at a comical scene, they are likely to grow into adults who are unable to express their emotions at all or unable to express them in an acceptable manner. Some may not be able to recognize their emotions. Teachers are in a position to have a powerful impact on the kind of adults youngsters grow up to be.

Most students can learn by open-ended questions as well as regurgitating details teachers have presented to them. There are often many acceptable answers to questions. Teachers should not expect students to give only answers that he or she had in mind. Encouraging students to express their own ideas and opinions and being accepting of them is a characteristic of humanistic education.

6. "Humanistic Education strives to develop learning environments which are perceived by all involved as challenging, understanding, supportive, exciting, and free from threat."

The goal of making learning a challenge is not synonymous with making learning hard or difficult. If students are provided with work that is at the proper level and is presented at the appropriate rate, it is a given factor that the material will be challenging. For instance, in the academic area of reading, a child's instructional level is estimated to be the point where he can read successfully 92 percent of the vocabulary words and can correctly answer at least 75 percent of the comprehension questions in a given selection. These percentages leave room for students to strive for 100 percent competency in vocabulary and comprehension. Thus, the material is within their ability, but, yet, challenges them to become more proficient in reading. If all subject areas were approached in this manner, learners could have the stimulation of striving toward complete mastery and, at the same time, feel successful.

Being understanding with students involves many processes, but one of the most vital of these is first to reach the student. The goal should be to develop a one-to-one relationship with each individual student. This may be accomplished by establishing good eye-contact, greeting each child at the door as he or she enters the classroom, or providing some time during the day for private communication with each student. Sending personal notes to the children or having a quick, undisturbed chat are other ways of contacting the students. Another major skill that goes along with understanding is that of listening to students. This includes such teacher behavior as listening without interrupting, facing the child speaking, and looking the child directly in the eye. These skills are particularly important when dealing with handicapped students who may have a disfiguring physical impairment or problems with speech. Students need to know that teachers are understanding of them and their difficulties.

Teachers may be supportive of students by believing that they are able, valuable, and responsible. By displaying this positive attitude students will come to realize that teachers do care about them and will give support not only in the learning process but in difficult situations.

Public law 94-142 helps project the feeling that students are able by placing them in the most appropriate educational setting. This is more commonly known as mainstreaming. Here, the schools are saying to educable handicapped youngsters that they are capable of successfully coping and interacting with their more normal peers. This was not true when the learners were isolated in self-contained trailers or rooms all day and were allowed little or no contact with regular class children.

Other situations that teachers may arrange to show support would be to expose youngsters of varying age groups to each other and to structure settings so that they may learn from each other. Assigning students specific jobs to do in the classroom each day is one way to begin teaching responsibility. Many handicapped youngsters need to be taught responsibility and need to have teachers who believe in their abilities.

Making school exiciting is indeed a challenge for all teachers. Many of our students are bored with the deluge of workbooks, ditto sheets, and dry approaches that are frequently used in our schools. Special classes are no exception. Often the dullness is expanded by such inappropriate tasks as requiring educable mentally retarded teenagers to complete endless color worksheets or string beads. Normal students as well as the handicapped are capable of learning through teaching approaches that encourage divergent thinking and creativity. Although mentally retarded children learn best through drill and repetition, subjects such as science and social studies lend themselves to more exciting approaches. Field trips, media presentations, interest centers, and active participation are some ways in which school may be made more exciting.

Developing a learning environment that is free of threat is difficult. Discipline is the one area that causes teachers the most problem. If teachers assume that students will act responsibly and treat them so, most students will respond in positive ways. By allowing youngsters to participate in making their own rules (making them fewer and more reasonable), by making the classroom as exciting as possible, by believing that students are basically trustworthy and by making sure that the students know that the teacher is fair, many discipline problems will be averted (Purkey, 1978).

Occasionally, pentalties will be necessary, but good discipline should be based on the contention that the student is an individual with dignity. Penalties for inappropriate behavior need to be discussed in advance, and these should be decided upon by both the teacher and students. Free access to support personnel such as the counselor, nurse, tutors, special education personnel, principal, etc., should be made available to the students. Atmospheres that denote threat and punishment only work to stifle democracy and learning. The goal should be freedom with responsibility.

7. **"Humanistic Education develops in learners genuine concern for the worth of others and skill in conflict resolutions."**

Before teachers can develop in students a concern for the value of others, they must believe that they themselves are deserving of respect, acceptance, and love. Positive self-regard on the part of the teacher is not an egotistical, selfish position. Rather, it is an honest and open appreciation of one's abilities and potential as well as the recognition of one's present limitations. It sets the stage for developing the same positive feelings in students.

One of the first things a teacher can do to foster concern for the worth of others is to be authentic with his or her own feelings. If a teacher does not like a child's behavior, being honest and telling the child is much better than smiling falsely to disguise true feelings. Teachers should tell their students when they are dissatisfied, not feeling well, or are busy.

Children also need to learn that teachers as well as other

students like to be treated nicely and that this usually causes a reciprocal reaction. Role playing activities, group discussions, and games about various types of feelings are ways in which this may be enhanced. In addition, teaching children to listen to others and to read body language is vital if they are to learn to value others.

Developing skill in conflict resolution may be more easily fostered by those teachers who employ such techniques as Reality Therapy (Glasser, 1965). Here the misdeed is identified by the student. A value judgement of the act is then made by the student along with a commitment not to let it happen again. The teacher's role is that of listening and guiding rather than condemning and punishing. Students should be encouraged to vent their feelings and frustrations before they get out of hand. When anger does occur, learning to talk it out or transfer hostility to sources such as a punching bag may help to prevent aggressive acts upon other students. Value clarification activities are found in such books as *100 Ways to Enhance Self-Concept in the Classroom, Values Clarification,* and *Developing Values with Exceptional Children.* These are excellent for developing conflict resolutions (Canfield and Wells, 1976; Simon, Howe, and Kirschenbaum, 1972; and Simon and O'Rourke, 1977).

SUMMARY

The learning objectives of the following vignettes are to provide through specific examples some measure of the breadth and depth of problems that teachers may expect to encounter with handicapped children of poverty and to stimulate the formulation of strategies for alleviating these problems. It is not possible, of course, in twenty or even a hundred case studies to exhaust the variety of these problems, but these examples have been chosen to provide an indication of the range that these may take. It does not take a long career in the public and special schools for teachers to encounter such a variety of problems. Most of these vignettes are drawn from six years of experience in such schools.

Few of us as teachers can be so callous as to ignore the problems that these students present. The vignettes are intended as an exercise in problem solving, so that, through group discussions in college classrooms and in workshops, teachers may engage in a free exchange of ideas. It is hoped that such discussions will help to provide a foundation of possible solutions that may be drawn on when similar problems are encountered in the practice of our profession.

Clearly, this author has a strong bias toward humanistic approaches in addressing such problems. It is certainly of interest to examine possible solutions, not only within the framework of the philosophy of humanistic education, but also from the standpoint of other educational philosophies as well.

Teachers, either consciously or unconsciously, develop an approach to teaching that influences the development of students as functioning human beings. It is hoped that the discussion of these vignettes with the associated questions will aid in the conscious development of a more successful approach to teaching.

REFERENCES

1. Allport, Gordon: *The Nature of Prejudice.* Cambridge, Addison-Wesley, 1954.
2. Bigge, June L.: *Teaching Individuals with Physical and Multiple Disabilities.* Columbus, Charles E. Merrill, 1976.
3. Canfield, Jack and Wells, Harold C.: *100 Ways to Enhance Self Concept in the Classroom: A Handbook for Teachers and Parents.* Englewood Cliffs, Prentice Hall Curriculum and Teaching Series, 1976.
4. Combs, Arthur W. (Ed.): *Humanistic Education: Goals and Objectives. Humanistic Education: Objectives and Assessment.* Washington, Association for Supervision and Curriculum Development, 1978.
5. Combs, Arthur W., Avila, Donald L., and Purkey, William W.: *Helping Relationships,* 2nd ed. Boston, Allyn and Bacon, 1971.
6. Dobson, Russell and Dobson, Judith Shelton: *Humaneness in Schools: A Neglected Force.* Dubuque, Kendall-Hunt, 1976.
7. Fantini, Mario and Weinstein, Gerald: *The Disadvantaged.* New York, Harper and Row, 1968.
8. Glasser, William: *Reality Therapy.* New York, Harper and Row, 1965.
9. Greenwood, Gordon E., Good, Thomas L., and Siegel, Betty L.: *Problem Situations in Teaching.* New York, Harper and Row, 1971.
10. Hall, Calvin S. and Lindzey, Gardner: *Theories of Personality.* New York, John Wiley and Sons, 1957.
11. Higgs, Reginald W.: Attitudes Formation—Contact or Information. *Exceptional Children,* 41: 96-97, 1975.
12. Maslow, Abraham H.: *Motivation and Personality.* New York, Harper and Row, 1954.
13. Maslow, Abraham H.: *Toward a Psychology of Being.* New York, D. Van Nostrand, 1962.

14. Passow, A. Harry, Goldberg, Miriam, and Tannenbaum, Abraham J. (Eds.). *Education of the Disadvantaged: A Book of Readings.* New York, Holt, Rienhart, and Winston, 1967.
15. Purkey, William W.: *Self-Concept and School Achievement,* Englewood Cliffs, Prentice-Hall, 1970.
16. Purkey, William W.: *Inviting School Success.* Belmont, Wadsworth, 1978.
17. Reisman, Frank: *The Culturally Deprived Child.* New York, Harper and Row, 1962.
18. Robinson, Nancy M. and Robinson, Halbert B.: *The Mentally Retarded Child.* New York: McGraw-Hill, 1976.
19. Rogers, Carl R.: Toward Becoming a Fully Functioning Person. *Perceiving, Behaving, and Becoming.* Washington, Association for Supervision and Curriculum Development, 1962.
20. Rogers, Carl R.: *Carl Rogers on Encounter Groups.* New York: Harper and Row, 1971.
21. Rogers, Carl R.: The Interpersonal Relationship in the Facilitation of Learning. *The Helping Relationship Sourcebook,* 2nd ed. Boston, Allyn and Bacon, 1971.
22. Rothstein, Jerome H.: *Mental Retardation: Readings and Resources.* New York, Holt, Rinehart, and Winston, 1971.
23. Simon, Sidney B., Howe, Leland W., and Kirschenbaum, Howard: *Values Clarification.* New York, Hart, 1972.
24. Simon, Sidney B. and O'Rourke, Robert D.,: *Developing Values with Exceptional Children.* New Jersey, Prentice-Hall, 1977.
25. Sims, William E.: Humanizing Education for Handicapped and Culturally Different Students. *The Journal of Professional Studies, 5:* 35-58, 1980.
26. Swanson, B. Marion and Willis, Diane J.: *Understanding Exceptional Children and Youth.* Chicago, Rand McNally, 1979.
27. U.S. Bureau of the Census: *Statistical Abstract of the United States,* 100th Edition. Washington, 1979.
28. Vogt, D.K.: *Literacy Among Youths 12-17 Years.* Washington, U.S. Government Printing Office, 1973.

EDDIE'S FINGER

M rs. Arnold had moved the previous day to this small, mountain community. Two weeks earlier she had accepted the position over the phone as a special education teacher for a self-contained class of intermediate age educable mentally retarded children. Because of this late committment, there had been no opportunity for her to become acclimatized to the community, school, or students.

The first day of school Mrs. Arnold was confronted with eighteen not-so-shining faces. The students ranged in ages from nine to fifteen, and with the exception of one or two, most looked as though they had come from extremely deprived homes. Five of them looked particularly ragged and dirty. As Mrs. Arnold checked their names on the roll, she discovered that they were all Gordons. She questioned them and discovered that, indeed, they were all brothers and sisters.

Mrs. Arnold began work that morning by administering an informal academic inventory test to the children. As midmorning approached, however, the children were becoming restless and uncooperative. It was apparent that few of them had eaten breakfast. By eleven o'clock it was out of the question to continue with the testing; thus Mrs. Arnold dispensed with it and drew the children together in a group.

She began talking about herself, giving them her background, family situation, etc., and then asked each child if he would like to tell about himself. Most were eager to share. Mrs. Arnold discovered many interesting and helpful facts about the lives of the children. The Gordons, for instance, lived in a remote section of the mountains and had to walk two miles to catch the school

27

bus. They also told her that they did not like school enough to walk that far; therefore, they were absent most of the time. This sharing session also helped to distract the youngsters from the growling of empty stomachs.

As lunch time approached, Mrs. Arnold lined the children in a single file, and they proceeded to the lunchroom. On the way they stopped by the bathrooms to wash their hands. Since most of the children were not very clean, the teacher felt that she should check hands to make certain that they had scrubbed off the top layer of dirt.

When ten-year old Eddie Gordon was asked to show his palms, he refused. At Mrs. Arnold's insistence, he extended his hands, palms downward. Becoming rather irritated, Mrs. Arnold grabbed both of his hands and turned his palms up in search of soil. To her amazement, she discovered that Eddie had extra fingers on each hand. They were approximately two joints long and were attached in line below his "pinky" fingers. They were limp, as the child had no muscular control of them. Mrs. Arnold said nothing, but immediately released his hands. Eddie hung his head, stared at his feet, and shoved his hands into the pockets of his tattered pants. Mrs. Arnold dispensed with the remaining hand checks and led the children into the cafeteria.

A few weeks later, Mrs. Arnold found herself settled and adjusted to the area. With the memory of the hand-check incident vivid in her mind, she had been making close observations of Eddie. The majority of the time the boy was quiet and with-drawn. He clung to his younger, nine-year-old brother, Johnny, who did most of the talking for the two of them. When Eddie did speak, it was evident that he had an articulation problem. It was difficult to understand him. Mrs. Arnold recommended him for speech therapy, which he received twice a week. Academically, he was reading at a 3.5 grade level, and his math was on the fourth grade level. Mrs. Arnold soon realized that Eddie was the highest functioning child in the class.

Mrs. Arnold was concerned about the lack of breakfast for the children; so she discussed the matter with her principal. He agreed to supply each child with a carton of milk in the mornings, but that was the extent of the school's contribution. Mrs. Arnold and her aide brought in boxes of cereal to give the children with the milk. With this nourishment, the children were able to work until lunch.

The teacher began making home visits, and thus, she got to know the parents on a more personal level. She was happily surprised at the Gordon's residence. It was true that the house was located on a back, mountain road, but it was small, white, and looked fairly sturdy. The family had electricity, but no running water. They used a nearby stream for water. There were, of course, no bathing facilities. Having no refrigerator, they kept perishable items in a spring house not far from their back door. The inside of the house was sparsely furnished, but what they had was neat and clean.

Will Harper married Dora Gordon soon after the death of her husband. It was also after the birth of her fourteenth child, Johnny. At this time, only the five youngest children remained at home along with three preschool grandchildren. The grandchildren belonged to an older, unmarried daughter. This daughter worked at a truck-stop on the interstate, and she claimed not to be able to care for her children. She paid her mother ten dollars a month for keeping them.

Neither Will nor Dora was in any physical condition to work. They subsisted on a meager amount of money Will received from a small government stipend. They did not get welfare money, food stamps, or surplus food. The family was extremely close-knit. Often the older children would come home to visit, but they were not much better off financially than their mother.

Mrs. Arnold got along well with Eddie's mother and step-father. She felt free to talk with Mrs. Harper about Eddie's extra fingers. The mother, too, stated that she was worried about Eddie's negative reaction to them. Two of her older children also had them, but neither were bothered by their existence. One of the girls was reported to have proudly shown them off. In addition, one of the younger grandchildren had the extra fingers. None of these children had been born in a hospital, thus there had been no opportunity to have them removed at birth. Mrs. Harper said that she would like to see them taken off in hopes of making Eddie happier, but she had no idea as to how to go about it. In addition, she emphasized that she had no money or transportation to assist with the surgery.

After the home visit, Mrs. Arnold sat down with Eddie and asked him how he felt about having his little fingers removed. His eyes lit up, and he said he did want them off.

In the meantime Mrs. Arnold began learning more about the community, its service organization, church groups, and state facilities. She kept in close touch with Dora and Will Harper and encouraged them to send the children to school regularly. Eddie and Johnny never missed a day, but the older children were frequently absent. When they returned to school, one would smile and say, "We had to help Mama with the babies."

The Gordons were in desperate need of clothing. Mrs. Arnold found a church group willing to collect clothes for them. Rather than bringing the clothes to school and allowing the children to take them home on the bus, one of the church ladies insisted on taking them directly to the Gordon's home "to see the look on their faces when I walk in with these things." Mrs. Arnold reluctantly agreed to take her. To the woman's disappointment, they showed no emotion. After several embarrassing minutes, Mrs. Harper finally thanked her and then chatted a bit with Mrs. Arnold. The lady was never seen again; however, the children wore the clothes every day.

By November Mrs. Arnold had arranged the surgery through the local health department. The operation was to take place in a city approximately seventy miles away, and the bill was to be paid by the Crippled Children's Association.

With the money the teacher had collected from the Jaycettes and business people, she bought Eddie a complete new outfit consisting of a blue suit, shirt, tie, underwear, socks, and shoes. There was money left over to get pajamas, which he said he had never worn before, two sets of school clothes for both him and Johnny, and a stack of comic books.

Because no one else was available to go, Mrs. Arnold took Eddie on the bus to the city for his surgery. He stood tall and proud in his new clothes as they walked from the bus station to the hospital, which happened to be only a few blocks away.

When they arrived at the hospital, they were faced with the unexpected hospital admittance rule. The hospital must have a parent's written permission before a minor could be admitted for medication and surgery. Mrs. Arnold's heart sank, but when she explained all of the circumstances to the person in admissions, she was told that they would accept a telegram from Mrs. Harper; however, it must be received by seven o'clock that night in order for the medical preparation to occur in time for the surgery. On the promise that the telegram would be forthcoming Eddie was assigned a room. Mrs. Arnold stayed with him long enough to see that he was settled. Since it was approaching four o'clock, Mrs. Arnold left to catch the returning bus.

After stopping at every small town along the way, the bus rolled into the station at six o'clock. Mrs. Arnold got off the bus, into her car, and raced the ten miles up the mountain to get Mrs. Harper. Together, they found a neighbor with a phone, and after some difficulty, managed to get the telegram off just in time. Mrs. Arnold fell into the bed that night, exhausted, but happy.

Eddie's surgery was successfully completed the next day. Two days later, Mrs. Arnold took Dora and Will Harper to the city to get him. When they walked into his room, he was wearing his new pajamas, sitting up in bed, watching television, and eating ice cream. Although his hands were sore and bandaged, he managed a big grin for his parents and teacher. They were unable to return him to the surgeon to have the stitches removed. Mrs. Arnold took him to a local doctor who removed the stitches and did the final check-up. There was no immediate change in Eddie after the surgery.

At Christmas time the class was asked to put on a play for the local chapter of the Council for Exceptional Children at a night meeting. Most of the children in the class eagerly participated, including the Gordons; however, as time approached closer for the play, the Gordons seemed less and less interested. At last Mrs. Arnold discovered that they were concerned about how they would get back into town for the play and home afterward. To relieve their anxiety, Mrs. Arnold invited all five of them to spend the night of the play with her. She made another home visit and got written permission for the children to stay with her.

The night of the play, she wanted the children to eat well, thus she prepared a roast along with green beans and a variety of other vegetables, but to her surprise, all they wanted were the brown-and-serve rolls. She had to send to the store for more before the meal was over. The play went quite well. The special class

children beamed when the audience clapped after their performance.

The next morning at breakfast Mrs. Arnold was making
conversation by asking the children what they usually ate for
breakfast. They all became silent, and in a minute the oldest boy,
who was fifteen, began looking around the table and answered,
"bacon, eggs, sausage, toast, and juice," Johnny looked over at
Eddie with his mouth wide open, grinned, and kicked him under
the table. Mrs. Arnold quickly changed the subject.

Later that week for a special treat the Jaycetts took the class to
eat lunch at the Tastee Freeze. Here, Mrs. Arnold discovered to her
surprise that many of the children had never eaten french fries or
had a milk shake.

When the Christmas holidays were over, Mrs. Arnold sadly
discovered that the Gordon children had moved. Losing five
students out of eighteen in the class certainly made teaching
easier, but the children were missed. However, one morning in
the latter part of March, the Gordons bounded into the room. All
five of them carried big smiles. They told Mrs. Arnold that they
did not like the other class and had insisted that Will move them
back to this school district. Since she had not seen their parents in
several months, Mrs. Arnold made another home visit. This time
they were living on a main highway in a gas station, which had
long ago been abandoned. They were thrilled with this place for
it had electricity, running water, and a toilet that worked, "if you
pour a bucket of water down it."

Earlier that year Mrs. Arnold had purchased a hair cutting kit
and had been cutting several of the boys' hair. They all wanted
crew cuts; so that became Mrs. Arnold's specialty. Hearing of this
and seeing the results on the boys, Will sent word for Mrs. Arnold
to please come and cut his hair. On this visit, she gave him a good,
short crew cut.

By the end of the year, it was obvious to all involved that Eddie
had had a personality change, since he "got his little fingers cut
off." He no longer hid his hands in his pockets or depended as
much on Johnny. His speech still prevented him from being a
talker, but he became more aggressive and joined in games with
the other children.

That summer, Mrs. Arnold moved to another town, but invited

Eddie and Johnny to visit with her for a week. She bought them new summer outfits, including swim suits. While visiting her, they went to see their first movie, swam in a real cement pool, and ate at a Big Boy restaurant. After three days, they began to question her about all the money she was spending on them. For the rest of the week she set up chores for them to do "to earn their way." At the end of the week, she returned them to their mother. That was the last time she had contact with the family.

Stimulus Questions

1. Was it important for Mrs. Arnold to share her background before asking the students to share theirs? Why?
2. How should Mrs. Arnold have reacted when hearing that the Gordons missed school, because they didn't like to walk so far to the bus?
3. Should teachers check on children's cleanliness? Why? Isn't this an invasion of privacy? .
4. Is it a teacher's responsibility to feed children at school? What else could Mrs. Arnold have done to get breakfast provided for the children?
5. What are the values, if any, of home visits?
6. What are the advantages of a teacher being familiar with a community in terms of helping her students?
7. Should Mrs. Arnold have taken the church lady with her to visit? Why or why not?
8. What is the medical name for Eddie's condition?
9. What was the purpose of Mrs. Arnold's collecting clothes and toys for Eddie when he went for the surgery? Was it necessary?
10. Discuss Mrs. Arnold's involvement with Eddie's surgery.
11. Why do you suppose Mrs. Arnold questioned the children about their eating habits when she knew they were poor? How did the children feel about her questioning?
12. How were the Gordons' values different from Mrs. Arnold's?
13. Should Mrs. Arnold have had the children to visit her that summer? Could such a visit make a difference in the boys' lives?
14. How would you describe the emotional climate in Eddie's home?

15. In what ways was Eddie deprived?
16. How do you suppose Mrs. Arnold's family reacted to her deep involvement with Eddie?

THE BIRD FELL OUT OF THE CAGE

E ight-year-old Dwight Ingram had spent the summer of 1970 in a demonstration school for educable handicapped children. The school was operated by the local university to give its special education students an opportunity to have hands-on experiences with children. The teacher was a woman who had many years of teaching experience, and she operated the class smoothly and efficiently.

This was an important time for Dwight. He had been classified as seriously emotionally disturbed and had caused such a problem in previous classrooms that the school system was on the verge of expelling him. At that time, the only existing program for emotionally disturbed youngsters was one at the middle school level, and, of course, Dwight was too young to be placed there. This summer school placement was his "last chance." If this experienced teacher couldn't cope with him, the school intended to refuse to accept him for the fall.

Fortunately, Dwight was able to adjust satisfactorily. There were only seven children in the class, which ran from nine o'clock until noon everyday. This situation, along with wise guidance from his teacher, provided Dwight with the support he needed.

The school system noted the boy's progress, and it was decided that Dwight would be allowed to attend their system in the fall. Since this summer class was temporary, the child was assigned to the new primary class for educable mentally retarded children. The summer school teacher was returning to college on a full time basis to pursue graduate work, thus a young woman, Mrs. Kendall, was hired to replace her. Mrs. Kendall had just received her master's degree in special education from the University, and, although she came with high recommendations, she had no teaching experience.

35

The new class was self-contained in one of the older, but elite, elementary schools in the city. This was the first year the school had been required to house a special class. There was a good deal of apprehension among the faculty. Most of the teachers had been in this school for many years and were accustomed to the children of university faculty.

The special class was assigned a large, end room. The buses could let the children out near the school entrance. This way the children could enter their classroom without walking down the hall. Across the hall and next door were the regular fifth and six grade classrooms. The children in these classes were busy and quiet most of the day.

The eighteen youngsters in the special education class ranged in age from six to ten. They exhibited a variety of handicaps. There were four disturbed children, including Dwight, two children with Down's syndrome, and one with moderate cerebral palsy. The others had a variety of physical and learning difficulties, and most, including Dwight, were from economically deprived homes. The children as a group were active and loud. This class would have been a challenge for even an experienced teacher with an aide, but a near impossible task for a first year teacher to handle alone.

Mrs. Kendall insisted on staggering the children's entrance into the classroom. The purpose was two-fold. One was to get to know the youngsters on an individual basis and to acquaint each of them with the physical setting of the classroom and school. The second purpose was to allow time to assess each child with the informal academic inventory.

When Dwight was brought into the classroom for this period, he was totally uncooperative. He wouldn't sit down to do the work, threw the pencil on the floor, and talked endlessly about his fantasies. He would go to the chalkboard and draw picture after picture of trucks. At last, when Mrs. Kendall presented him with a sheet of addition facts, his eyes lit up, and he sat down and began to answer the problems without hesitation. His mathematical ability was astounding for an eight year old. He eagerly worked his way through addition, subtraction, multiplication, and division. However, he would have nothing to do with reading, spelling, or phonics. Mrs. Kendall decided to postpone that section of the evaluation. She made arrangements to visit with him in his home later that week to try to complete the testing.

Dwight's home was an old, wooden, white house beside a large shopping center. In spite of the decaying conditions of the house, it was spotless and neat inside. He lived with his parents and a younger brother and sister. An older sister was married to a military man and was living out-of-state.

Mrs. Kendall was greeted warmly by Mrs. Ingram and was offered a soft drink. She accepted and sat and talked with Dwight's mother for a while. Dwight stood in the doorway of the living room and listened to every word. Mrs. Ingram stated that the only person who could handle Dwight was her married daughter. When Mrs. Kendall asked how this was done, Mrs. Ingram smiled sheepishly, shrugged her shoulders, and did not verbally respond.

Dwight and Mrs. Kendall soon went into his bedroom to complete the inventory. The room contained three beds that were crowded together. They sat on one of the beds and began to work. Mrs. Kendall was able to get him to respond to the phonics test and the reading vocabulary word list. He refused to attempt the reading paragraphs or spelling sections. When presented with these, he crawled under the bed. With the results she gathered, it appeared that Dwight was reading at approximately the second grade level.

The first two weeks of class were uneventful. The children were busy adjusting to a new school, a new teacher, and, in most cases, new classmates. For the most part, the children were cooperative, and it looked to Mrs. Kendall that the year would go smoothly.

During the end of the third week, however, Dwight began going to the blackboard and drawing pictures of trucks, as he had done that first day. He explained them loudly to the class, saying they were moving vans, milk trucks, and trucks bringing toys to stores. Each day the trucks grew larger and more numerous, until finally, Dwight would enter the classroom, go to the board, and proceed to fill up every available space with trucks. No amount of cajoling, threatening, or distracting would pry him away from this activity. Just as Mrs. Kendall started to panic, Dwight stopped his drawings and returned to his seat to complete his work.

Mrs. Kendall was a staunch believer in immediately reinforcing the children's work as they completed it. She managed
this by circulating around the room and visiting each child at his
seat every five minutes. Dwight, however, insisted on coming up
to her while she was instructing groups in reading or math. He
demanded that his paper be graded at this time, thus interrupting
the group lesson.

Once in early October Mrs. Kendall refused to allow him to
interrupt and ordered him back to his seat. Dwight fell on the
floor on his back and began to kick, scream, and thrash around.
The other children remained in their seats with all eyes fixed on
the screaming child. After hearing the noise, the fifth and sixth
grade teachers rushed in to the room to find Mrs. Kendall
standing over the hysterical Dwight. She assured them that the
situation was under control. With puzzled looks on their faces,
the teachers returned to their classroom.

After a few minutes, which seemed like hours to Mrs. Kendall,
the boy suddenly stopped screaming, calmly stood up, and said to
Mrs. Kendall, "The bird fell out of the cage." The class appeared
to be in a dazed state the remainder of the day. From then on,
about every other day, Dwight's "bird" would fall out, and he
would have another temper tantrum. The class was under
constant tension, wondering when it would happen again.

Another incident which caused Mrs. Kendall to wonder about
Dwight's placement involved his behavior during lunch. The
school lunchroom was located in the auditorium beside the stage.
One day Dwight decided that rather than eat at the table with the
other children, he would take his tray up to the stage and eat
there. When he wouldn't respond to verbal instruction, Mrs.
Kendall went up to him, took his tray away, and placed it back on
the table. Dwight reluctantly went back to the table to eat.

On the way back to the classroom, Dwight got on all fours and
began going down the hall barking like a dog. The children in
the regular classes wanted to see what was making the noise, thus
they clustered in their doorways. Dwight was doing a perfect
imitation of a dog. When he wasn't barking, his tongue was
hanging out, and his bottom was wagging an invisible tail.

To get him to enter the classroom, Mrs. Kendall held his resting
mat on the floor in front of him and slowly drug it into the room.

Dwight, the dog, went after the end of the mat, batting it with his "paw." When Mrs. Kendall had both the mat and Dwight inside the room, she quickly shut the door. Dwight got on his mat and went to sleep. When he awoke, he was Dwight, the boy, again.

The last straw occured the last of October when Dwight stood up in front of the class, pulled down his pants, and began to urinate on the floor. Mrs. Kendal called his mother, told her what had happened, and asked her to come and get her son.

Twenty minutes later Dwight's older sister appeared at the door of the classroom. She was a masculine-looking woman who wore jeans and a plaid shirt. She stood with her legs apart and firmly planted to the floor. In her right hand she carried a wide leather belt which had been doubled over. Dwight took one look at her and froze. His eyes were wide as he stared at the belt. With a great deal of reluctance he left the room with her. Everyone knew what was in store for him.

Mrs. Kendall stayed at school that afternoon and had a conference with the principal. It was decided that the teacher should write a detailed description of Dwight's behavior while in her classroom. This, in turn, was to be submitted to the school board. The school board unamiously agreed that their system was not able to cope with a child of Dwight's problems. He was, therefore, not allowed to return to school.

Mrs. Kendall felt frustrated and was deeply concerned about Dwight; however, she felt her first responsibility was to the other seventeen children in the class. They needed her time and attention.

Months later, Mrs. Kendall discovered that Dwight had been sent to live with his sister in another state and had been attending a private school there. There was no future report on his progress.

Stimulus Questions

1. What do you think would have happened to Dwight if his last chance had failed?
2. Should Dwight have been assigned to the special class with an inexperienced teacher and no aide? Why?
3. What can schools do to help introduce "special classes" to the other faculty members? How can special education teachers

ease the fears of regular class teachers about handicapped children?

4. Should severely disturbed children attend class half day or all day long?

5. How can early home visits help a teacher learn about a child? Will this help in setting up a program for the child?

6. What types of acting out behavior did Dwight exhibit? Does stopping this behavior mean that he is cured? Why or why not?

7. Was the sister's way of managing the child helpful for Dwight's problem? Why?

8. Why did Dwight do the work in his home that he had refused to do in school?

9. Why did Dwight suddenly stop spending all of his time drawing trucks?

10. How do you think Dwight's tantrums affected the performance of the other children?

11. What could Mrs. Kendall do to help the other students adjust to Dwight's noisy behavior?

12. What kind of reinforcement was he receiving for his acting out? Could this be controlled?

13. Was the school system within their rights to expel Dwight for his behavior? Support your answer.

HONESTY IN THE LUNCHROOM

O nita and her younger brother often rode in the back of their father's dilapidated, but functioning, truck. Mr. Hart was aware of the danger of the children being in the back. They were not allowed to stand up or move around while the vehicle was in motion. Even with this precaution, Onita was injured when the truck went out of control and crashed into the concrete median. The girl's left leg was crushed. Fortunately, the leg was saved, but it was broken in several places, and the muscles and ligaments around her foot were torn. Mr. Hart and Onita's brother escaped with no more than a few bruises.

Because of the degree and severity of her injury, Onita was sent to a special orthopedic center where surgery was performed. Here, the broken bones were set in the leg, and the bones on the side of her foot were stabilized together. The latter had to be performed, because the muscles that controlled the turning movements of her foot were severed. By stabilizing these bones, the foot would remain in a straight position without the use of muscles.

Onita was eleven years old and in the sixth grade when the accident happened. She was a nice looking child with long, dark hair, chocolate-brown eyes, and olive skin. She was outgoing and friendly, and although not a leader, she got along well with her peers. As a student, she was not outstanding, but she did above average work in areas that required reading. Math had always caused her considerable difficulty.

The Hart family consisted of poor, but hardworking, people. Mr. Hart was a farmer. He owned and farmed several acres of land that had always been in his family. Mrs. Hart worked as a cleaning woman for five families each week. Their cash income together was not much, but with the farm, they always had enough to eat. In addition to her parents and Onita, there were three younger boys who made up the family.

Onita remained in the hospital for three months and when she returned home she wore a long-leg brace and crutches. It was now December and approaching Christmas vacation at school. After the holidays, she returned to her sixth grade classroom to complete that year.

The youngster had received a good deal of attention from her classmates. They had all sent a continuous stream of letters, cards, and gifts to her, and many had even visited her in the hospital. In essence the peer bond had been kept up. Onita was happy to return to school, although she knew she would be behind academically. Some effort had been made in the hospital to continue her education, but she had progressed little, particularily in math.

She had been placed in a combined fifth and sixth grade classroom at the beginning of the year. The principal decided it would be best to let her return to the same setting rather than place her in the other sixth grade classroom in the school.

The teacher, Mrs. Matthews, became pregnant in October, and, although she was a veteran teacher of ten years, she began to feel bad and often grumpy and showed uneven temperment with the children. She was determined to finish out this year of teaching, have the baby the next summer, and return to the classroom in the fall. The woman was not prepared to handle children who required special attention. There were thirty-four children in the room and, in addition to Onita, there was a boy with severe asthma problems. The class also had its usual bright children, slow learners, behavior difficulties, and a class clown. The setting was far from ideal, especially when the teacher was experiencing an uncomfortable pregnancy.

After a few weeks, Mrs. Matthews began to secretly wish that Onita had not been placed back into her room. Not only was the child behind in her work, but she had become accustomed to receiving attention from the doctors, nurses, and her parents. Onita continued to expect the same from Mrs. Matthews. To complicate matters, Onita began to feel an admiration for her teachers. She wanted so badly to please Mrs. Matthews, but did not know how to go about accomplishing this. Onita would go up to Mrs. Matthews desk to ask for help, to show her a picture she had drawn, or for any other numerous reasons. Rather than gaining the teacher's approval, the child received short, terse responses, or reactions such as, "See me later," or "Can't you see I'm busy now?"

Onita knew that she was unable to gain positive attention through her academic achievements, thus she concentrated on her crafts. Each afternoon the class would participate in an hour-long arts and craft period. For one project, each child got a partner and shared a paint-by-number scene with the use of oil paints. Onita's partner was Herbie Watson, and they selected a picture of a Chinese junk. Herbie's hand-eye coordination left much to be desired, and Onita was not the neatest child in the world. Their finished product looked as though it had been done as a finger painting rather than with brush and oils. Mrs. Matthews displayed all of the painted scenes on a table in front of the room and then proceeded to award a prize to the best. Jill Jones and Sissy Camp won.

The next art activity was making string puppets. Onita spent hours gathering materials together at home to make the puppet. For a head, she found an old wooden ball. The idea was good, but her puppet's head was too heavy, and kept falling into its own lap. Jill Jones and Sissy Camp each won a prize for the best puppet.

Mrs. Matthews read to the class each day, and after completing the book, *Caddie Woodlawn*, she had each child make a book containing magazine pictures which represented people, scenes, and activities in the story. Since the children were to bring in their own magazines, Onita had to get some from neighbors. Her family did not have money to subscribe to such things. Her pictures were good representations of the story. However, the glue kept spilling out from under the pictures, and she ended up with sticky pages. They dried, and when pulled apart, many pages tore. Jill Jones won the prize. Sissy Camp had been absent with the chicken pox.

Finally, the day arrived when the biggest craft project was to take place. Each child was allowed to select a rubber mold into which plaster-of-paris was poured. Onita's greatest enjoyment was to watch old cowboy movies, thus she selected a cowboy mold. Three times she carefully poured the plaster-of-paris into the mold to harden. And three times the cowboy's head broke off as she peeled back the mold. Mrs. Matthews was exasperated with Onita at this point. The youngster was given only one more chance. Again, the head broke off. Onita was handed the glue and told to glue the head to the body. When the product was complete, the head was tilted to the side, excess glue was abundant around the neck of the cowboy, and the tempera paint had run down from the red shirt to the blue pants. It was, indeed, an unusual creation, but Onita was proud of it.

All of the plaster-of-paris models were displayed on the table in the front of the room where they were viewed for several days. Then came the time for the announcement of the winner. Onita was breathless with excitement as Mrs. Matthews stood up to identify who had won. Mrs. Matthews first described the winner's product. The colors were vivid, the painting immaculate, the mold perfect, the choice of subject was brilliant, and the winner was Sissy Camp, who had made an angel in prayer. Onita experienced the same let-down feeling as she had on so many other occasions, but Jill Jones cried. She had made a butterfly and felt that its quality was as deserving as the angel in prayer.

Onita was coming to realize that she was not exactly Mrs. Matthew's favorite pupil. She was made to stay after school many days to have special help with multiplication and division. When it was obvious that Onita was still experiencing difficulty even on a one-to-one basis, Mrs. Matthews' tolerance was quite limited. She yelled at the child more than once that she had never seen anyone so dumb in math. Onita would just sigh and hang her head.

The youngster's relationship with the other children was also becoming somewhat limited. They all liked her. She had a keen sense of humor and thoroughly enjoyed their antics. On the playground, however, the boys went to one corner and played ball, and the girls were involved in such active games as jump rope, hopscotch, tag, etc. Because of her leg, Onita was only able to play on the merry-go-round or with the swings. Here, she made friends with some of the quieter children, but having been active and on the more aggressive side she felt isolated from her old friends.

Before the year was over, Onita developed a friendship with Sissy Camp. This was the first year the girls had been in the same room. Although they did not play together at recess, Sissy often went home in the afternoon with Onita. Sissy was an extremely bright child and did more than anyone to help Onita "catch up" in her schoolwork. She explained that fractions were as easy as "sliding off a greasy log." She also had wisdom and compassion beyond her years and saw the difficulty Onita was having with Mrs. Matthews. Sissy didn't know how to advise her friend, but her support certainly aided Onita through that year.

Mrs. Matthews decided one day that the children were wasting too much food in the lunchroom. She began to require that each child bring his plate to her to be checked, before they would be allowed to leave. Recess followed the lunch; so the children were all eager to get out of the lunchroom. Onita had never been much of an eater, and the school lunches were not exactly her idea of what should constitute a meal. Her least favorite lunch consisted of over-cooked navy beans, slaw, cornbread and a three-by-one piece of cheese which flopped back and forth when held up. It was chewy and difficult to swallow.

Onita knew that she would never pass the "clean plate test." She began giving away food to some of the hungrier children. Mrs. Matthews quickly put an end to this. Onita spent many afternoons sitting in the lunchroom staring at a cold plate of food. Indeed, she not only missed recess, but much of the afternoon's instruction.

In desperation, the youngster began searching for places to hide the food. Wrapping some in a napkin and holding it under the plate while being checked proved successful, as did putting food in the milk carton. On a few occasions, Onita put the beans in the shoe of her weak leg. Since she used crutches, she could swing the leg along without putting pressure on the shoe, and thus not make a big mess. She would then go to a water spigot outside the building and wash out the beans.

Mrs. Matthews realized that many of the children were not really eating the food. She established an "Honesty in the Lunchroom" chart that was placed on a wall in the back of the room. When the children were honest about eating their food, they were to put a star beside their name. Each day Onita would come up and put a star in the proper position. The child tried harder to eat the food, but with little degree of success. She gave up and continued to smuggle it out.

When the teacher realized her system had failed, she spent one solid hour lecturing her students about the pitfalls of cheating. Being an extremely religious woman, she explained to them that the person who was cheating was headed for Hell in the next life. Onita was so troubled that she found herself barely able to breathe. As she sat in her seat, she felt herself being split. Her body felt as though it were coming apart. The guilt was almost unbearable. Mrs. Matthews finished her lecture by saying that the guilty person could attain forgiveness by apologizing to her and then to the entire class.

Later that afternoon, during crafts, Onita went up to Mrs. Matthews' desk and stated, "I'm sorry I did what I did in the lunchroom today." Mrs. Matthews smiled and nodded to her. "I'll apologize to the class when they aren't busy," the child went on to say. "I'll tell you when," said Mrs. Matthews. Onita waited, but the teacher didn't call on her. She spent a restless night and waited in agony the second day. At afternoon recess Onita began talking with the other pupils about the incident. Each child she asked was also waiting. As it turned out, half the class had admitted guilt to the teacher. No one was called upon to apologize. The chart came down quickly, and there was no more mention of "honesty in the lunchroom."

The students in Mrs. Matthew's class learned the words to many songs which they would remember for years to come. Such songs as "Bless this House," "Beautiful Dreamer," "Little Brown Church in the Dale," and "Oh, Holy Night." Mrs. Matthews would write the words of each new song on the board, the students would copy them, and the class would sing the songs together. Onita looked forward to this part of each day.

For the last month of school Onita dreaded to get her report card, for she knew Mrs. Matthews did not like her. She was fearful that the teacher was going to make her repeat the sixth grade, not only because of her poor performance in math, but also because of the cheating incident. She was pleasantly surprised when she received a "D" in arithmetic and was promoted to the seventh grade.

Stimulus Questions

1. What services could have been provided to make the transition from the hospital back to the classroom easier for Onita?
2. Did the principal make a wise decision about placing Onita back into the same classroom in which she began the year?
3. What assistance could have been given Mrs. Matthews in coping with a child such as Onita?
4. Should Onita have remained in this situation? Explain.
5. How could Mrs. Matthews have better handled Onita's need for attention?
6. How do you feel about Mrs. Matthew's judging the children's crafts? Why do you suppose she continued to allow one or two children to consistently win?
7. What could have been done to assist Onita with her arithmetic difficulties?
8. How could Onita have been included in some of her friend's activities?
9. What would have been a more humanistic approach to discourage the children from wasting their food?
10. How do you feel about Mrs. Matthews moralistic approach to the cheating episode? How else could this have been handled?
11. What positive aspects do you see in Mrs. Matthew's teaching?
12. What could have prevented Onita's last minute anxiety over passing the sixth grade?
13. How could the incidences that Onita endured in the sixth grade affect her in later life?

THE MOTHER'S PLAN

G atestreet Middle School was the latest addition to the southern town's public school system and all of the sixth, seventh, and eighth graders attended classes here. It was in its second year of operation.

Mrs. Jackson was one of the two special education teachers. Her classes were set up on a resource room basis so that the educable mentally retarded children attended in various time blocks according to their needs. Most of them were in Mrs. Jackson's class for at least two hours a day. Three could not function in the normal setting and were with her all day.

One of the students who was newly assigned to Mrs. Jackson's resource room for part of the day was thirteen-year-old Karen Pugh. Karen was a carbon copy of Elizabeth Taylor. She was small in stature, had dazzling blue eyes, and long, thick, jet black hair. Her skin was creamy and smooth. She was a sweet, happy, and extremely cooperative girl. She wore tight fitting sweaters over well-developed breasts along with above-the-knee length, loose, cotton skirts.

Her problem lay in two major areas, language development and academics. Although her speech was clear, her language was similar to that of a three-year-old child. She spoke in short, hesitant sentences, and consistently substituted the pronoun, "me," for "I," for example, "Me want to eat." Karen's IQ was approximately 60. After her academic evaluation, it was discovered that her reading was on the second grade level, and she was just beginning to learn addition and subtraction facts in arithmetic. Because of her level of functioning in these areas, Mrs. Jackson scheduled her to be in the resource room three hours per day to receive assistance in reading, arithmetic, and spelling.

48

Karen's attendance the first two weeks of school was perfect, and, when she did not appear for two consecutive weeks, Mrs. Jackson became concerned. The teacher had planned to make home visits in the near future, but she decided to go early to Karen's home to determine the reason for the girl's absence.

The Pugh family lived on a paved street in a low-income, but not poverty stricken section of town. The houses in the neighborhood were small, wooden, and fairly well kept.

Since few of the houses had numbers, it was necessary to stop at a neighbor's house to ask directions. A lady came to the door, smiling, but when the Pugh name was mentioned, the woman frowned and reluctantly pointed out the house. Mrs. Jackson understood why the woman was perturbed as she turned in the direction of the Pugh residence.

Karen's house was quite small, one room in width, and was covered with black tar-paper. The tar-paper was attached to the basic structure with one and one-half inch silver, circular disks which were nailed vertically in rows at approximately seven inch intervals. There was one slender tree in the tiny front yard. Dirt and sand made up the yard with exception of a few small clumps of tall weeds scattered about the front and sides.

Mrs. Jackson tried to park her car on the side of the street, but ended up with two wheels in the yard. As she got out of the car, she realized that there was no front door or screen, only a direct opening into the house. A large rock had been placed in front of the opening as a step into the doorway.

The teacher knocked on the door frame, and immediately a huge disheveled woman appeared. "What do you want?" the woman asked gruffly. Mrs. Jackson replied that she was Karen's teacher and that she wished to talk with her about Karen's schooling. "Karen ain't going to no school," said the woman. "May I please come in and talk with you about it?" responded Mrs. Jackson. At that moment Karen appeared from a back room and begged her mother to talk with the teacher. The mother hesitated, then motioned for Mrs. Jackson to enter.

The room appeared to be the living area, but the only sitting space was one twin bed and an old stuffed chair. A television was located on a table at one end of the room. The place was cluttered with newspapers. Mrs. Jackson sat in the chair, and Karen and her mother sat on the bed.

Mrs. Jackson began the discussion by saying how much she enjoyed having Karen in class and that she knew Karen could learn more with the proper instruction. She then asked the mother why she did not want Karen to go to school. The mother replied that she was waiting for the girl's "blood" to start so she could put her with men and make money. The woman expressed concern that at thirteen, Karen had not yet began her menstrual period. She asked the teacher if she thought there was anything wrong with Karen. Trying not to show shock and at the same time breathing through her teeth so as to avoid swallowing one of the hundreds of flies in the room, Mrs. Jackson answered that it was not unusual for a girl to begin her period at thirteen or even later. She also suggested to the mother that she take Karen to a physician for a physical examination to make certain there was no problem.

Karen's mother listened quietly to the teacher, then stated loudly and firmly, "I don't believe in doctors no more," She went on to explain that her son, who was two years older than Karen, had died of a ruptured appendix three years earlier.

The teacher interpreted the story to mean that the family had waited until the last minute to summon the doctor, and by the time he arrived, the boy's appendix had ruptured. Although he was taken to the hospital, it was too late to save him. "Them doctors are 'sposed to know how to save people, but they just let my boy die. Ain't no other young'un of mine going to be looked at by one of them quacks," stated the mother. "I'm keeping Karen at home 'till that blood comes, and she can be put with men where she's a belonging to be."

Swatting at the flies crawling over her face, Mrs. Jackson suggested that since Karen had not yet started her period she be allowed to return to school until it did appear. In the meantime, she argued, it would give Karen a chance to improve her reading and arithmetic skills. Not wanting to give in, the girl's mother replied that she needed Karen to help with the gardening. "Don't you think she could do it after school?" said Mrs. Jackson. "The gardening season is about over." Karen, who had been silent throughout the conversation, began pleading with her mother to let her return to school. With a sigh, the woman gave in to the argument by saying, "I reckon she can go. She does need to learn more. She ain't done so good in school. Learning is hard for her.

But she's got to be with you all day." Mrs. Jackson agreed, and the mother promised that Karen would begin school the next day.

Karen did continue with school that year and did not miss a single day. Mrs. Jackson saw to it that Karen learned not only academics, but the girl was taught the facts of life, including birth control measures.

Karen did not return to school the next year, so Mrs. Jackson turned the matter over to social services, hoping that the year she had spent with the girl proved beneficial in some way.

Stimulus Questions

1. Why did Karen's mother object to her attending school?
2. Should Mrs. Jackson have made a home visit to check on Karen's absence after only four days?
3. Why do you suppose Karen begged her mother to speak to Mrs. Jackson?
4. Should Karen's mother be reported for child abuse?
5. Should law enforcement officials be made aware of Karen's mother's plans for her daughter?
6. Is Mrs. Pugh's reaction typical of someone in her socio-economic status?
7. What should be done to educate people about health and family services?
8. Why do you think Mrs. Pugh let Karen return to school? What does this tell you about Mrs. Pugh?
9. What is the school's responsibility regarding teaching sex education to children? Should MR children be taught sex education? What should be included?
10. What should be the role of Mrs. Jackson; teacher/social worker or only teacher? How can this role be clearly defined?
11. How aware do you think Karen is of her situation and the future her mother has planned for her?
12. Do you think one year will make a difference in Karen's future? Explain.
13. What do you think the focus of Karen's education should have been during that year?

THE THROW-BACK

In the year 1910, Doctor Hunter P. Collinsworth established his medical practice in a small town. He had graduated with honors from medical school and was eager to begin his practice. Although he was an excellent physician, he had one major weakness. He loved women, all women. He was a good-looking, dashing fellow who won the hearts and bodies of many women before moving on to others.

It was not long before his reputation had spread throughout the town. His practice quickly became limited to men, and the socially acceptable families would not let him near their daughters.

Soon one of the women with whom he had been having sexual relations became pregnant. She threatened to accuse him publicly and ruin his practice unless he married her. He complied, in order to salvage what little remained of his work. This woman was from a low-income family. In addition, the family members had a history of mental illness, mental retardation, and physical handicaps. The woman, herself, was mentally unstable.

After the marriage, Doctor Collinsworth provided the woman with as much domestic help as she needed to keep the household functioning. He attempted to demonstrate to the citizens of the town that he was happily married. Indeed, after the child, a boy, was born, his medical practice improved. Two years later, Mrs. Collinsworth gave birth to a daughter. By now, Doctor Collinsworth had established himself as one of the leading physicians of the area.

For nine years Doctor Collinsworth's home life centered around his son. The boy went everywhere with him. He was a bright and interesting child, much like Doctor Collinsworth.

52

Tragedy struck when, at nine years old, the boy accidentally hanged himself while playing with a rope. Doctor Collinsworth threw himself into his work and seldom was seen at home.

The daughter proved to be as emotionally unstable as her mother. Her teachers suspected that she was mentally retarded. After the girl grew into puberty, she became as sexually promiscuous as both of her parents had been. When Doctor Collinsworth realized the situation, he had the girl escorted to school and locked in her room at night. When she was sixteen, however, she became pregnant in spite of the precautions. She did not know who the father was, thus marriage was out of the question.

Doctor Collinsworth died of a heart attack soon after the birth of his grandaughter, Clara. He lived long enough to see that his daughter became sterilized.

Mrs. Collinsworth, her daughter, and baby Clara lived together in the house provided by Doctor Collinsworth for five years. At that time the daughter became dissatisfied with this arrangement and demanded to move out. She and her mother had begun having arguments over the men that visited them.

The daughter and little Clara moved into the servant's house next door. Mrs. Collinsworth had fired the domestic help after Doctor Collinsworth's death; so the smaller house was vacant. It was a small, white, three-room house that had a tiny porch on the front and a fireplace in each room. Both houses were becoming filthy and run-down.

Doctor Collinsworth's daughter continued her active sex life away from the confines of her mother. Clara grew up with memories of endless men filing in and out of the house. Mrs. Collinsworth became more and more emotionally unstable, until finally, she committed suicide when Clara was twenty. Doctor Collinsworth's original house was beyond repair. It sat in a run-down condition.

Clara continued to live with her mother. Men stopped visiting as often, for the older woman was no longer appealing to them. Clara, herself, had never shown a particular interest in men. She was brighter and more stable than her mother, but they both continued to live in poverty. Doctor Collinsworth's money had long ago been depleted.

At age twenty-eight Clara married Mr. Barnett, a man much older than herself. He did odd jobs around the town and had been in the community for only several months when he met and married Clara. Having no real home of his own, he moved in with Clara and her mother.

Within five years Mr. Barnett and Clara had produced four children. The father couldn't take the bedlam in the small house, so he left. He would reappear occasionally with a few dollars, but he had no influence over the children.

Raeford was the oldest of the four children. He was a handsome child who resembled Doctor Collinsworth. He had been born at home after a long, hard labor. From the beginning, Clara noticed that he favored his right side, and this became increasingly more apparent as time went on. When the child tried to crawl, he would pull himself along with his right arm, push with his right leg, and drag the left side of his body. Clara watched him with concern, but did not know where to turn for help.

When Raeford wasn't walking at three years and his younger sister was ambulatory at fifteen months, Clara took him to the local health clinic for his first physical examination. The physician there explained to her that Raeford was suffering from cerebral palsy, and that it was unlikely he would ever walk unassisted. The boy's speech was slightly impaired but not enough to prevent him from communicating efficiently.

Raeford was referred to both a speech therapist and a physical therapist. Clara took him to see each one a couple of times, but with her family expanding and no means of transportation, these visits soon stopped. The physical therapist did show Clara several exercises to do with Raeford's weak leg, and, to her credit, she performed these religiously. In spite of the physician's prediction, Raeford, at age six, did walk unassisted, but with a severe limp.

The large, yellow bus stopped in front of the Collinsworth house to take Raeford to his first day of school. The boy had turned six in May, and he had been eagerly awaiting the opening of school. With some difficulty, the child climbed the tall steps of the bus unassisted.

Upon arriving at school Raeford was taken to Miss Pansy's first grade classroom. Miss Pansy had been teaching for twenty-six years. She had never married, and had dedicated her life to teaching. The one thing she had never grown accustomed to, however, was unclean children. She was a believer in the old saying, "Cleanliness is next to Godliness." Her philosophy was practiced in quite a blunt manner. Miss Pansy took one look at Raeford and said, "Well, I can see you are poor and crippled, but you don't have to come to school smelling like a pole cat." Surprised at that remark, Raeford's bright, eager eyes filled with hurt. He immediately cast them down to the floor. "Don't stand there like a knot-on-a-log. Find a seat and get in it," continued Miss Pansy. The child obeyed and quietly slid into a seat, hunched up his shoulders, and tried to make himself as unobtrusive as possible. He could not control the hot tears that filled his eyes and rolled down his cheeks.

Thus began Raeford's school career. He somehow survived the year with Miss Pansy in spite of her rude and thoughtless comments. He had inherited Doctor Collinsworth's strong academic ability and he was able to learn quickly and efficiently. This surprised Miss Pansy, and she remarked to another teacher in Raeford's presence that he must be a "throw-back" to his great-grandfather.

In his early grades, Raeford was tolerated, if not accepted, by his classmates. As the students grew older, however, Raeford's ragged clothes and smell of urine from sleeping with younger children became offensive to them. The boy's physical disability prevented him from participating in the active playground games. He spent most of his time on the swings or merry-go-round.

Raeford wanted more than anything to be able to play baseball, but the few times he attempted it, he struck out so often the boys wouldn't allow him to play. Many days he would go off alone behind school, face the wall, and cry into the crook of his arm. Other days he would wait alone at the back of the school entrance. When questioned by his teacher as to why he always played here alone, Raeford explained that he merely wanted to be the first in line into the classroom. She made no other effort to incorporate him into the group activities.

After school, he played with an old softball he found in a vacant lot. He would throw it up against the wall of his great-grandfather's house and practice catching it as it bounced back. His one great dream was to be allowed to play baseball with the other boys. He wanted to make homeruns or be the best pitcher around. He avoided going home into the filth and bedlam by staying out until dark, even in the cold winter months.

By the time Raeford was twelve, his school life remained lonely, and his home was in an almost unbearable state. His grandmother was old, sick, cranky, and demanding. She did nothing to contribute to the food preparation, cleaning, or other household chores. Clara was becoming more like her mother each day and was providing less and less for the children. The three younger children roamed the town unsupervised and were known as the town urchins.

At age fourteen Raeford was hired to work at the local tannery each day after school and on Saturdays. The work consisted of sweeping up the pieces of leather that fell during the cutting process. It required a good deal of stooping and bending which Raeford managed to do, but it didn't help his physical condition. His back was weak, and the work left him extremely tired. However, with the money he earned he was able to provide the family with a little extra food. With a portion of the money the boy had his clothes sent to a laundry. Each morning, he tied up his dirty clothes in a small bundle and put it on the porch for the laundry truck to pick up. He continued this practice throughout high school.

At school Raeford continued to be at the top of his class academically. He was still shunned by most of the other students and was considered to be weird. His interest in baseball remained, and he wanted more than anything to be on the school team. Of course, his physical problems and job did not allow this to be.

No one in his family came to Raeford's graduation, but to his surprise and pleasure, he was awarded a partial college scholarship. He selected a small, church sponsored school near his hometown and found a job there to help cover his expenses.

As usual, he did well academically, but socially, it was difficult for him. The other students teased him and made jokes about his clothes and appearance to such an extent that he was considering withdrawing from college. Raeford had made one close friend, and this boy convinced him to stay. This friend told his family about Raeford's plight, and they provided him with some decent clothing. This helped immensely, and Raeford graduated with honors from the small school.

Raeford went on to medical school and returned to his hometown to practice. He met Miss Pansy on the street one day and she remarked to him, "Why, if it isn't little Raeford Collinsworth. I always knew you would make something of yourself, thanks to all that good teaching you had in your early years." "Yes, Miss Pansy," Raeford replied as he walked on down the street, "Whenever I felt like quitting, I remembered your class."

Stimulus Questions

1. Is Raeford's family history of instability, mental illness, mental retardation, and physical handicaps important information for his school to know?
2. Was Doctor Collinsworth justified in having his daughter sterilized? Should people who are mentally retarded be sterilized? Explain.
3. How could Clara have learned about help for her child who was not progressing normally?
4. Did Miss Pansy's experience give her the right to demean a student for his lack of cleanliness? How else could she have handled his problem?
5. How could the school have prepared Raeford's teacher for his problems before he came to class?
6. Is Raeford unusual in his ability to overcome the odds and learn in spite of his unhappy situation? How do you think he did it without any support?
7. What could Raeford's teacher have done to include him in the play activities of the other children? Should she have done anything?
8. What do Raeford's actions tell you about his self-concept?
9. What do you think he wanted to do with his life?
10. What kinds of counseling programs should colleges provide handicapped students?
11. Why did Raeford go back to his home town to practice medicine?

LULA BELL'S SEXUAL EXPLORATION

L ula Bell Wehunt never uttered a word when she was in the
resource room. She entered each day with a dazed look in her
eyes and a pout on her lips. She would slip into a chair, sit on her
lower spine, and only half-heartedly attempt to do her work. She
sat in this position even during the instructional part of the
period.

This tall, lanky, twelve-year-old always wore one of two short
dresses tied with sashes in the back. Each day she wore red or blue
tights and the same sweater, which she kept buttoned up the
front. The sweater had large holes at both elbows. Lula Bell's
clothes were usually clean, however. She had fine, straight blonde
hair that was cut short in back, but hung in bangs at eye level in
the front.

Mrs. Wehunt had been an active lady wrestler when she became
pregnant with Lula Bell. She was three months along before she
realized her condition. Only then did she stop participating in the
wrestling events. By that time, the damage to Lula Bell had been
done.

Lula Bell appeared normal at birth, but it was soon apparent to
the mother that the child was lagging behind in her physical
development. The youngster was a year old before she could sit
alone. She didn't begin to crawl until sixteen months, and she
didn't walk until age two. In addition, her language development
was far below that of children with similar chronological ages.
The mother had two girls older than Lula Bell, so she was aware
of the differences between this child and her other youngsters.

Mrs. Wehunt was busy the next few years having two other
children. She wrestled occasionally, but only at night when her
husband was home. Lula Bell did not receive a preschool

58

educational experience. The child spent these years at home staring at a blaring television set.

When Lula Bell began first grade, the teacher soon recognized that the child was behind in all areas of development. She was quiet and withdrawn, consequently the teacher often over-looked her. There were thirty-four children in the class, and they all demanded a great deal of the teacher's time. Lula Bell seemed content to sit at her seat to wait until the teacher came to her.

This school situation continued until Lula Bell had repeated the first, second, and third grades. Her last third grade teacher was appalled that the child could have been ignored for five years. She quickly requested that the youngster have individual assessment. During the evaluation it was reported that Lula Bell wasn't totally cooperative. She responded in almost inaudible whispers and refused to answer many of the verbal questions. Her IQ was derived to be 58.

The placement committee for the school met, and after examining the data, recommended that Lula Bell be placed in the special class for educable mentally retarded children. Mrs. Wehunt had been called in for a conference even before the intelligence assessment, and she was willing for her child to attend the special class.

Since the girl had been left behind by her peers, it was decided that she should remain in the special class for all academic subjects. Her other time would be spent with children in the regular fifth grade.

Lula Bell remained in the special class for the next two years. Under the guidance of the special education teacher, the girl's reading level improved to the third grade, and in math she was functioning at the second grade level. The teacher felt that Lula Bell could have done better in her academic work if it had not been for her attitude. She was still quiet, but as she had grown older, she began to pout and frown with an over-all negative outlook. Often she refused to do any work. She would merely sit and stare at her papers. She never laughed or smiled and had no friends.

Lula Bell's seventh year in school brought forth new problems. She was now attending the middle school, where she continued to receive academic assistance from the special education teacher,

Mrs. Harper. Again, she spent most of the day in the special class. Her new teacher was kind and interested in the girl. The teacher spent time talking with her and trying to get her to respond, but to no avail.

Several weeks after school began Mrs. Harper noticed that Lula Bell had turned her desk facing the back wall of the room. When the teacher went over to determine the reason, Lula Bell quickly pulled her hand out from the inside of her tights. Mrs. Harper said nothing, but convinced the youngster to turn her desk around and continue with her lessons. This activity continued to occur each day, but only in the special class. At last Mrs. Harper decided that a talk with Mrs. Wehunt was in order; so she set up a time to visit at their home.

The Wehunt family moved around the town a great deal, living in trailers and run-down apartments. At this time they were living in an old, rock house beside the train tracks. Mrs. Wehunt was a large, muscular woman who looked as if she could protect herself in any situation. Mr. Wehunt wasn't at home during Mrs. Harper's visit. Mrs. Wehunt referred to him as "that skinny, worthless, old man." He was working at odd jobs, but not making enough money to get the family off welfare. Mrs. Wehunt stated that she was thrilled to get him out of the house for awhile. All of the children were at home and sat listening to the conversation.

Mrs. Wehunt began talking about Lula Bell's schooling problem and volunteered her reasoning for the cause. The mother stated that when she was wrestling one of the other lady wrestlers consistently kicked her in the abdomen. This treatment occurred several times when she was pregnant with Lula Bell. Thus, Mrs. Wehunt blamed "that blond, curly, headed bitch" for Lula Bell's learning difficulties. The mother went on to say that she did not wrestle anymore, although they needed the money. She explained that she couldn't trust the older girls to be at home at night without her. She had caught both of them having sex with boys outside of the house, when she had left them alone. She said she was afraid they would get "knocked-up," and she would have to raise their babies.

Noting the roughness of the mother, Mrs. Harper was reluctant to bring up Lula Bell's masturbation problem, but felt that she must do so. To the teacher's surprise, Mrs. Wehunt responded calmly. She told Mrs. Harper that this had been going on a long time at home and that was why Lula Bell always wore tights, "to make it harder to get to." The mother also said that she had tried every way she could think of to break her of this habit, including putting red hot pepper on her fingers and tying her hands behind her back. She swore to Lula Bell that if it ever happened at school, she would "beat the hell out of her."

Mrs. Harper immediately regretted mentioning this to Mrs. Wehunt and tried to smooth things over by saying it had only happened once and that it could be handled at school. The teacher saw that her plea was falling on deaf ears, for Mrs. Wehunt was giving Lula Bell a vengeful eye. Mrs. Harper left feeling like nothing had been accomplished, and indeed, that Lula Bell was worse off.

The youngster returned to school three days later even quieter and more sullen than before the home visit. For about a week there was no sign of the masturbation, then one day the old routine returned, and, again, it was limited to the special class. This time Lula Bell made no effort to hide herself. Mrs. Harper began to ponder over what her next approach should be.

Stimulus Questions

1. What could Mrs. Wehunt have done when she first became aware of Lula Bell's problem? What are some of the possible causes of the child's masturbation?
2. What kinds of early experiences are available for children of lower income families?
3. Is it unusual for a quiet child to be ignored by teachers who are coping with maximum numbers of children in their classes?
4. How could Lula Bell's lack of progress have been noticed before the third grade? Who should be noticing these problems?
5. Was it helping Lula Bell to spend most of her time in the special class and not with her peers?
6. Why do you think Lula Bell had such a negative attitude?
7. What could be done to promote her interest in school and making friends?

8. How did Mrs. Wehunt's attitude toward her husband affect the other children?
9. What do you think Mrs. Harper should do about Lula Bell's problem of masturbation in school? Where could she go for help?
10. Do you think that Mrs. Harper or Mrs. Wehunt should be the one to handle the problem?
11. Would sex education for the class be beneficial? Why?

A LIMITATION, BUT NOT A HANDICAP

Lavern's early years were rather uneventful. Her parents were poor tenant farmers in the South who planted the land and picked the crops, which consisted mainly of cotton. There had been nine children born into the family and seven were living. Lavern was the fourth in line.

Although quite low on the financial scale, they resided in a rather old, but roomy, well-insulated, white house. This was unusual for tenant farmers in the area. The house had no indoor plumbing. They used an outhouse and got their water from a well. In the eyes of their neighbors though they were considered well off. Both parents were hardworking people who managed to keep the children clean, clothed, and fed. They canned food from a huge garden in the summer, and this got them through the winter. The mother had a sewing machine and made most of their clothes.

In addition to the immediate family, there were many aunts, uncles, and cousins living nearby. They were close-knit and would visit frequently during the week. On Sundays all of the family gathered at the local Primitive Baptist Church to attend the two-to-three hour service. If weather permitted, they had a picnic in the church yard under large, old, shade trees. Food was abundant here, and they would sit, eat, and visit all afternoon. Then, they would reenter the church and participate in another two hour service. Religion infiltrated their lives. As a result, Lavern's parents were strict, but loving.

Lavern's Uncle Frederick was one of the strong leaders in the community, because he owned his own land. Also, he was a brilliant man who knew how to manage money well enough to live comfortably. He had always taken a particular interest in

Lavern, for he could see early that she too, was exceptionally bright. He spent many hours playing with her and reading to her. Although her home had few books, he would purchase inexpensive ones for her at a dime store.

Two of Lavern's aunts were totally blind and were dependent on the family to "do" for them. In addition, Lavern's older sister, Rebecca, had begun losing her sight at age seven. Now, at twelve, she too, was totally blind. Rebecca had not been very bright in her school work. Her parents removed her from school and were trying to teach her to help out with the farm chores.

In the second grade, Lavern discovered that in order to see the blackboard, she had to sit on the front row. When her parents purchased glasses for her, the children teased her and referred to her as "four eyes." By the time she began third grade, her vision was deteriorating so rapidly that she could no longer see the board, and letters on her paper had to be three inches high. It was apparent that she was going blind.

Her third grade teacher was helpful and read her work to her. In the fourth grade, however, her teacher was not so understanding and simply allowed her to sit alone for hours. She was reportedly even rude to the child and obviously didn't want to be bothered with the extra work Lavern required.

When Uncle Frederick was told of the situation, he was quite upset. He had insisted that Lavern remain in school rather than being taken out like Rebecca, and the idea that the school wasn't helping her infuriated him.

About this time another incident happened which frightened the family. Lavern was struck in the head with a baseball bat at school. The boys had moved the base to an area of the school yard where Lavern was sitting and when a boy swung at and hit a ball, he threw the bat back toward Lavern. The bat hit her head, knocking her out. The school was apologetic to her parents, but they did not know how to cope with Lavern.

At Uncle Frederick's suggestion, Lavern was sent to the state school for the blind at the beginning of her fifth grade. Being from a close family and never having been away from home before, Lavern's adjustment was less than satisfactory. At first, she withdrew to her bed and refused to even eat. At the threat of being fed intraveneously, she did pick up her eating habits. At the school, they made little or no effort to place the students with roommates of the same age, thus Lavern ended up with a fifteen-year-old girl. The girl had her own friends, and Lavern continued to be quite lonely. After several months, with her quick mind, she was able to learn braille.

When she went home at Christmas, she begged her parents to let her stay, but thinking of her future, they insisted she return to the state school. The next summer, she was so insistent on staying home that they became tired of arguing with her and agreed to put her back into the local public school for her sixth grade.

Lavern had learned personal independence at the state school at a crucial time. By now, she had only a little side vision. She could make out human figures, but could not tell who they were.

Her sixth grade teacher was an older woman, Mrs. Lennon, who had been teaching for twenty-five years. She was quite willing to have Lavern in the class, but had no idea of how to go about teaching her. Since there were no special school services, Mrs. Lennon was alone in her planning.

The day before school was to begin, she sat down to have a talk with Lavern in hopes of discovering a key to help her. She wanted to determine her academic level of functioning. Mrs. Lennon discovered that in spite of her intelligence Lavern had lost a complete academic year in school. Evidently, she had spent the entire fifth grade becoming proficient in braille rather than keeping up with her academic work. Mrs. Lennon considered the possibility of telling this to the principal, but decided to hold off and see how fast the child could catch up. Also, she was visited by Uncle Frederick who offered to order all of Lavern's books from the Institute for the Blind. They agreed to do this, but in the mean time, Lavern needed to begin work.

In the classroom, Mrs. Lennon seated Lavern beside her desk near the board, and although she couldn't see, she would not miss any of the discussion. Next, she asked for volunteers from the other children to read all of Lavern's work to her and write down her answers. At first, the children were reluctant, but when they realized that those who read were given special treats, such as extra milk, they began to volunteer and actually argue about whose turn it was.

Homework posed a problem, for none of Lavern's family really cared about reading or, truthfully, was able to handle sixth grade material. Mrs. Lennon, herself, offered to work with her on the assignments after school each day. As it turned out, Lavern's bus was the last to leave; so this gave them the necessary time. After a month, Mrs. Lennon was seeing the effort pay off. Lavern was learning quickly and flying through the material. After six weeks, the braille books came, and work began in earnest.

Socially, however, Lavern still encountered problems. Even though the others were willing to help her with work, no close friendship bonds were being formed. It seemed they still considered her an odd girl because of the blindness. Mrs. Lennon overheard one boy teasing her and saying, "Well, you aren't old four eyes anymore, you're just a blind bat." In a rage, Mrs. Lennon jerked him up and gave him a firm paddling, but this did not stop the teasing and insults after school. One day in December when Lavern was ill and absent from school, she had a talk with the class. She tried to explain to them about Lavern's handicap in a factual kind of way, she ended up by pleading with them to be kinder. This worked to some extent, but the lack of empathy was still apparent.

Soon afterward, in desperation, Mrs. Lennon decided to play a game with the class. Half of them were to wear blindfolds for an entire school day and pretend they were blind. They were assigned a seeing student and were to depend on that person all day. The next day, those who had been blindfolded were allowed to see, and the others were made to wear the blindfolds. It worked like magic. Afterward, in the class discussion, some tears even flowed. They finally realized what Lavern's problem was like and, in turn, were much more sympathetic and helpful with her. Some parents had their complaints, but were calmed down when the reason behind the blindfolds were explained to them.

With Mrs. Lennon's help, the class ended the year with a closeness that continued to exist throughout high school. Lavern graduated valedictorian of her class and won a scholarship to college, where she achieved a 4.0 average. She was planning for a teaching career to work with other blind students.

Stimulus Questions

1. In what way did her uncle's encouragement influence

Lavern's academic success?

2. Why was the fourth grade teacher not willing to help Lavern? Should the school have taken some action with this attitude problem?
3. Was the school for the blind good for Lavern in spite of her longing for her family? Explain.
4. Why was it important for Lavern to be in a room with someone her own age? How did this affect her later ability to make friends?
5. What kind of teacher was Mrs. Lennon? What did she value?
6. Why were the children reluctant to have anything to do with her?
7. Why did the beginning methods used by Mrs. Lennon to enlist empathy for Lavern not work?
8. Do normal children need to experience new things in order to fully understand them? Do you agree with the drastic measures Mrs. Lennon finally took to try to change the student's attitudes? Why?
9. What other empathy-building activities could the teacher have used?
10. Was the unity of the class an important factor in the success that Lavern finally enjoyed? Why?

THE BULLY

W ayne Rogers was nine years old. He was a handsome child with dark brown eyes, brown hair, and a smooth, olive complexion. He had even white teeth, and when he smiled there were dimples in each cheek. Every day he wore tight fitting blue jeans and a red and white, striped, knit shirt. He was always clean and neat.

At the beginning of his school career, Wayne had been placed in a class for the educable mentally retarded. Four years later he still remained in the special class and was functioning academically on the latter part of the first grade.

This year Mrs. Howard was the new special education teacher. She avoided looking at her children's permanent record files at the beginning of school, except to check their medical records. She was aware of the self-fulfilling prophecy and did not want to be influenced by other teacher's comments.

Mrs. Howard and Wayne started off the year with good rapport. Several of the other children in the class required a great deal of individual attention. Thus, Wayne was left to work alone much of the day. He did, however, participate in academic group instruction. He volunteered to help around the room, and Mrs. Howard came to rely on Wayne. The first few weeks he appeared to be a model student.

Mrs. Howard encouraged all of the children to get their parents to the first PTA meeting. They made attractive invitations and discussed the meeting in detail. In spite of these efforts, not a single parent attended. The next day Mrs. Howard told the children how disappointed she was that no one had come. With that remark, Wayne's hand shot up, and he stated that, indeed, his mother was at the meeting. Mrs. Howard felt badly that she had not seen the woman to welcome her.

The teacher soon started visiting the homes of her students. Many of them lived in one particularly poor section of town. The Harley Drive area consisted of one long, twisty, unpaved road lined with many small, run-down, unpainted houses. A few had tiny yards with grass, a tree or two, and perhaps a fence, but the majority were built up next to the road.

Wayne lived on Harley Drive. His house was one of the last on this dead-end street. It was quite shabby, unpainted, and unstable looking. As Mrs. Howard approached the house, she noticed that there were no windows or doors. The dirt yard did have several big shade trees.

Wayne was wearing ragged shorts and a dirty, white tee shirt. He stood behind one of the large trees, partially hiding himself. His two brothers were playing on the ground with an old rusted truck. All three children smiled shyly at the teacher as she passed them.

Wayne's mother met Mrs. Howard at the door and asked her to come into the house. Mrs. Rogers was a tall, attractive woman, but much too thin. Wayne bore a striking resemblance to her. Mrs. Howard was invited to sit on the sofa. There, she began a conversation with Mrs. Rogers about Wayne. One of the questions Mrs. Howard asked was how Wayne was disciplined at home. Mrs. Rogers tucked in her head, looked down at the floor, and replied, "Sometimes I have to put him in the closet." The teacher was surprised at this response, but tried not to show it and did not pursue the topic any further. Conversation was difficult, for Mrs. Rogers did not communicate spontaneously. However, Mrs. Howard was able to gain useful information about Wayne. She also discovered that the woman had not been to the PTA meeting.

Before Mrs. Howard left, she was invited into the one bedroom to see the Roger's three-month-old baby girl. Since the family had had three boys first, Mrs. Rogers seemed especially proud of this child. The baby was sleeping in a large wooden box, which had been placed on the seats of two chairs. The box had been lined with soft, pink sheets, and a pink blanket. As far as Mrs. Howard was able to determine the baby was normal and healthy.

Approximately two weeks later, Mrs. Howard noticed that

Wayne was extremely restless in the classroom. He worked for only a few minutes at a time, and then he got up and wandered around the room. In the beginning he would fidget with the pencil sharpener, objects on the desks, books, games, etc. Gradually, this was transferred to other children. He would walk up to them in their seats and quickly punch their arms, pull their hair, or hit them in the back. On the playground this aggressive behavior was even more pronounced. He would shove, kick, or sock other children to the point of real pain.

By November, Wayne was the official class bully. He was a problem child both in and out of the classroom. If the other children were building a structure, one could count on Wayne to zip by and kick it apart. His physical attacks continued. They occurred without warning, and were seldom provoked. Wayne did not seem angry and appeared indifferent to the pain he was causing his victims. It was impossible for the other children to ignore him. He was so active and destructive, he seemed to be in two places at once.

Mrs. Howard tried many different techniques to cope with Wayne's problem. Talking with him about his aggressiveness was impossible. He would nod his head up and down and say, "Yeh, yeh, yeh." Appealing to his value system was futile. After one of his attacks in the lunchroom, Mrs. Howard, in desperation, grabbed him by the arm, dragged him to the room, and proceeded to spank him with the flat of her hand. He was even more aggressive that afternoon.

Mrs. Howard tried to build up the child's self-image by praise and attention. Wayne was always the first to volunteer to take the lunch money to the office, so, gradually, that became his job. In November, the principal reported to Mrs. Howard that money from the room had been missing for several weeks. They suspected that Wayne had been taking it. Thus, Mrs. Howard found it necessary to let other children carry the money.

Wayne was proud of two things. One was the fact that he brought in his lunch money every Monday morning. He would strut up to the teacher's desk and proudly place it in front of her. He did this in such a way that the other children could see that he was paying for the meals and that he was not on the free lunch program.

The other thing that brought pleasure to the boy's life was his baby sister. He talked about her incessantly. The class was kept notified of her latest developments.

After several sessions with the principal about Wayne and his problems, it was decided that he needed a time-out place in which to work. This was both for Wayne and the other children. Very little academic work was being accomplished in the room when Wayne wasn't receiving individual or group instruction. It was arranged that the youngster was to go to the principal's office to work each morning after his group instruction. He was to stay there until his work was completed. Only then was he allowed to return to the classroom. Also, the principal and Mrs. Howard decided that Wayne was to remain in the office during one recess period. He would be given another time to play, alone, when a teacher was free to take him out.

It was obvious to the school personnel that Wayne was an emotionally ill child who needed help. He was referred to a nearby center for evaluation and diagnosis. Indeed, the report on him confirmed the school's feelings. He was referred to a counselor in the community for therapy. Fortunately, Wayne's mother was willing to let him go, but the school had to provide him with transportation to the sessions.

The counselor made one new recommendation for Mrs. Howard. This was to provide rewards for Wayne when he was good in the classroom. Good was defined to Wayne as not making another child cry during the day. Mrs. Howard was given money by the school system to buy toys as a reward.

The first day the procedure went fine. Wayne was quite well behaved. He received a baseball at the end of the day to take home. After that, whenever he earned a toy, he would make a big production of giving the toy away to another child. A couple of weeks passed, and his behavior had, again, deteriorated so badly that the reward system was discontinued.

At mid-year Mrs. Howard decided to look at Wayne's past school history to see if his behavior had changed recently or if he had had a history of aggressive behavior. As she read the comments of other teachers, she saw the pattern was repeating itself. One teacher even ended her description of Wayne with the statement, "My hair has turned gray over this child."

In February Wayne came to school telling that his mother had "run off" with his baby sister. Mrs. Rogers had left Wayne, his brothers, and his father. This departure had a detrimental effect on Wayne. He came to school filthy and, in addition to his aggressiveness, he was extremely nervous. Fortunately, Wayne's mother returned to the family a month before school was out for the summer.

This school year came to an end with no child being hurt seriously. This was due to the cooperation of the principal, who allowed Wayne to stay in her office so much of the time.

The following school year, Wayne was placed in a newly formed one-half day program for emotionally disturbed children. Later that year Wayne's family moved away. There was no follow-up on his school career.

Stimulus Questions

1. What is an emotionally disturbed child? How was Wayne disturbed?
2. What is the self-fulfilling prophecy?
3. What are the advantages and disadvantages of not checking children's permanent record folders? Should Mrs. Howard have looked sooner? Why or why not?
4. How do you feel about the way Mrs. Howard handled the PTA incident? Why didn't the parents come?
5. Why do you think Wayne was so well behaved in the beginning? What do you think triggered his change?
6. How would you describe Wayne's self-concept? On what do you base this?
7. How do you think Wayne felt about his physical home environment?
8. What effect could putting a child in the closet have? Why do you suppose Mrs. Rogers treated Wayne in that manner?
9. Why do you think the "baby sister" was such an important element in Wayne's life?
10. What other behavior management techniques could Mrs. Howard try with Wayne?
11. Should the stealing and lying be considered a part of Wayne's emotional problem? Why?

12. Why did the reward system fail? What could be done to make it more successful?
13. What do you think Wayne's potential for a normal life would be without adequate therapy?

HELP FOR THE HUGHES

F reddy Hughes was born at home. He was delivered by his grandmother, who was the local mid-wife. This particular birth frightened the woman, for in all of her years of "birthing babies," she had never seen a child such as Freddy. He had an open place on his spine in which all of the nerves were exposed. In addition, his head seemed excessively large in proportion to the rest of his body. The front part of each foot was turned in severely toward the midline.

Although the family was quite poor and no member had ever been to a hospital, Freddy's grandmother was fearful that the child would die without medical help. She convinced the parents to let her take him there. He was examined promptly by a physician and diagnosed as having spina bifida with accompanying hydrocephalus and clubfoot.

It was too early to determine the extent of brain injury, but immediate surgery was indicated. The bulging sac of nerves on his spine needed repair, and the hydrocephalus condition had to be arrested before any further brain damage occurred. This surgery was performed when Freddy was only a few days old. Both corrections appeared to be successful.

Although his legs and feet were badly twisted, corrective surgery for this condition was delayed until the child was a year old. Until that time his feet were in casts and braces to prevent the condition from becoming worse.

Six years passed, and it was time for Freddy to begin school. His intelligence quotient was found to be 65 on an individually administered intelligence test. The child was placed in the first grade, but he attended a resource room for most of his academic instruction. He was classified as educable mentally retarded with an accompanying physical disability.

Although Freddy's hydrocephalus had been successfully arrested, the spina bifida and clubfoot conditions caused the youngster to need long leg braces. He could walk unassisted with the aid of crutches.

Freddy's family was crowded into a three room apartment in an old tenant house. The apartment was on the seventh floor. The stairs up the seven flights had long since lost their guard rails, and there was no form of lighting available in the stairwell. Paint was peeling off all the walls.

The boy's home-life left much to be desired. After Freddy, two more children had been born into the family, giving a total of nine offspring. Freddy's parents were both in ill health, and neither was capable of holding a job. The mother was particularly in bad shape. Having the nine children had drained her physically. Carrying the babies, including Freddy, up seven flights of stairs had permanently injured her back. She was, therefore, in pain much of the time. She was ill-tempered with the children and often resorted to harsh physical punishment.

The father, who was thirty-eight years old, had suffered one heart attack and, in addition, had high blood pressure. By trade he had been a carpenter's assistant, but because of his illness, could no longer work. The family subsisted on disability payments and food stamps.

Mrs. Clements was Freddy's first grade teacher. She was disturbed about his frequent absenteeism, thus she decided to make a home visit to determine the reason. Since the family lived in an extremely rough, unsafe neighborhood, she took one of the larger male members of the school faculty along with her for protection. This was desirable, even in daylight hours.

They parked on the street and were somewhat disgruntled about the way the children climbed all over the car as soon as they stopped. Children were playing everywhere, even in the street. The sidewalks were lined with full garbage cans, and many had been knocked over by the children. Trash covered the sidewalks and spilled over onto the street.

As the two teachers pulled up the long flight of stairs, they marveled that any of the children from the area survived the dangers of this environment. They noticed that the noise level was extremely high. Television sets were blaring; mothers were yelling at children; babies were screaming; and they even heard the residents arguing as angry voices echoed through the dark halls.

They reached the Hughes' apartment out of breath and had to stand and gasp for air before knocking on the door of the apartment. They were invited into the apartment by Freddy's mother. Except for the older children, all of the family members were present.

The living area was a dark, sparsely furnished room. The pungent odor of urine was almost intolerable. Although it was daytime, the only light came from a battered, black and white television set. Freddy's mother raised one of the crumbing shades to let in more light, but no one made an attempt to turn down the loud volume of the television set.

Freddy was seated in the only stuffed chair in the room and brightened up considerably when he saw the teachers. The two smaller children were quietly munching on saltine crackers. Both parents offered their straight-back chairs to the teachers. The other children were seated on the floor.

The teachers discussed Freddy in terms of his absences. His mother explained that this was due to their living accommodations. She was in so much pain from her back that she wasn't able to carry Freddy down the long flight of stairs each morning to catch the school bus. The father of course, was unable to do any lifting because of his heart problem. There was simply no one available to get the child to the bus.

Another problem was also brought out. The apartment had no bathroom. They had to walk down the long, dark hall to use one shared by several families. It was located too far for Freddy to walk, and if his mother was unable to carry him, he was forced to use a slop jar. He hated that, for it only got emptied once a day and wasn't comfortable. He was not able to urinate standing up. Therefore, he usually just wet his pants. The teachers promised to look into this matter, thanked the parents, and left. They were impressed with the interest both parents showed in Freddy.

Mrs. Clements could see no solution to the family's dilemma short of relocating them to a more convenient apartment. She began by visiting social services. She explained the family's plight to the proper officials. They were sympathetic, but gave little encouragement. The low rent housing development had a two year waiting list. Even considering the fact that they had a handicapped child, it would be at least a year before the family could be considered.

Frustrated, but still determined, Mrs. Clements went to the school principal to discuss the problem. The principal, too, agreed that the family must be moved, if for no other reason than to insure that Freddy received an education. Several other faculty members became interested in the situation, and they met as a group several times to offer suggestions.

The group, after exhausting every possible state agency for assistance, decided to take matters in their own hands. They discovered that one of the teachers owned a small apartment house about two blocks from the school. One of the three bedroom apartments with a bath had recently become available for rent. The problem of getting Freddy's family relocated there, consisted of a $200 deposit and fifty dollars a month higher rent than what they had been paying.

The group had discussed the move with Freddy's parents. They were eager to get out of their location. However, as the group of teachers suspected, the family was unable to come up with the deposit, nor were they able to spend an additional fifty dollars a month for rent.

After the family's plight was explained to the general faculty, donations were made, and the deposit was collected. The principal had been searching for another part-time maintenance man in the school. After talking with Freddy's father, he was given the job. This provided the family with the additional income needed to cover the rent.

Two faculty members volunteered to help the family move. Since the apartment had its own bathroom, Freddy could go alone to the toilet. The school's special mini-bus picked him up at the front door each day, and he began attending school on a regular basis. Mr Hughes worked out well with his new job. Nothing delighted Freddy anymore than to have his father come into the special classroom, even if it was part of his job. With Mr. Hughes' sweet temperament and easy going manner, he quickly became all the children's favorite maintenance man. He always had a smile and a pat for each one.

Freddy thrived in the new living conditions, and the regular meals he got at school were helping to improve his physical development. Mr. and Mrs. Hughes adjusted well to their surroundings, but Mrs. Hughes continued to have pain with her back. Since she could not afford medical care, she was forced to live with the discomfort. Otherwise, their situation was vastly improved by a few caring people.

Stimulus Questions

1. How could the unsafe conditions of the apartment building be improved? Who's responsibility is this repair?
2. Do you think the appearance of a male faculty member who is not Freddy's teacher could be a threat to his parents during the home visit?
3. How much effect do the conditions of a neighborhood have on the child's school performance?
4. Is it typical for parents of a handicapped child to take such a special interest in and be so concerned for their child?
5. Should Freddy's family be given special consideration by social agencies because of his handicap?
6. How can schools promote faculty interest and concern in students, handicapped or normal? Do you think the interest in this case was unusual? Explain.
7. How did the new job for Mr. Hughes affect his relationship with his family as well as Freddy?
8. What do you think will be the long range effects of this solution?
9. Do you think a family such as this could function in a modernized home? What kinds of assistance could be provided to teach the family the proper use of appliances, cleaning, etc.?
10. What could physical therapy have done for Freddy's condition? Where could he have gone for this?
11. Where could Mrs. Hughes have gone for medical attention for her back?

THE STUDENT TEACHING EXPERIENCE

N ancy Higgins was assigned a student teaching position in New Hampshire Elementary School in a fairly large metropolitan area. She was completing her degree in learning disabilities from one of the smaller universities. This was her last semester before graduating. Nancy felt that she had received excellent preparation in her courses for teaching children with learning handicaps; therefore, she entered the student teaching situation with enthusiasm and confidence.

Nancy's university felt that students in special education should have exposure to both normal and handicapped children. A student teaching situation was formulated that placed its students seven weeks in a regular classroom and seven weeks in a special class or resource room setting. Nancy was to begin her experience in the resource room for the initial seven weeks.

The student teacher arrived at the school the first day to face a dismal, dilapidated, three-story building that served as the elementary school. She felt her stomach "knot up." However, she swallowed and plunged ahead to the experience. The resource room was located on the top floor. In spite of the shabbiness of the building, the room was filled with interest centers located around the walls. Mrs. Datsun was the supervising teacher. A friendly relationship quickly developed between the two of them.

The first morning Mrs. Datsun explained about the youngsters who attended New Hampshire. Many were children of parents who worked at the local fabric mill. The other students came from a poverty-stricken community, which was located five miles from the school. Since many of the learning disabled students were from the latter area, Mrs. Datsun promised home visits for

79

Nancy with several of those students. The children who attended the resource room were in grades one through six, and they were twenty-five in number.

In the period before lunch, five sixth-grade boys were scheduled for reading. They were all dressed in their ragged clothing, and all were lean and undersized for their chronological ages of twelve to fifteen. When lunchtime approached, Mrs. Datsun sent them outside to play rather than taking them to eat. When Nancy questioned this, she was told that the principal had caught them smoking in the boys' restroom and for punishment had taken away their free lunches for an indefinite amount of time. Nancy was shocked at the cruelty, and before she had even met the man she decided that they would not have the best of relationships. When they encountered, she proved to be cool and indifferent, especially when she saw from his girth that he had apparently never missed a meal.

Mrs. Datsun proved to be an excellent model for Nancy. The methods she used were similar to those Nancy had learned in college. Things progressed smoothly along those lines. Mrs. Datsun planned the home visits soon after the student teaching session began. She felt that Nancy would have a deeper understanding of the children if she saw their home environments, particularly those from the deprived area.

Nancy became intrigued with a little seven-year-old boy named Bill Frank Parker. He was one of the younger children who attended the resource room and was also one of the children from the poor area. Bill Frank never initiated a conversation with anyone, but he would answer when spoken to with slow, hesitant speech. The youngster sat as far away as he could from the other children in his group. His eyes had a dazed, glassy look, and there would be times when he would become totally immobilized. Other times, he would concentrate on his work and complete it.

Bill Frank appeared to be an unkept child, and many days his body odor was offensive to those who sat hear him. He had big, blue eyes, sandy hair, and a ruddy complexion. His test results showed his intelligence to be in the low-normal range, but, academically, he was just learning to read, and his math was still in the readiness stage.

Nancy was eager to visit all the homes, but Bill Frank's

residence was her top choice. She and Mrs. Datsun sent notes home to alert the parents of their impending visit. No responses were returned, thus they made firm plans to go on the following Thursday after school.

The big day arrived, and the weather turned out to be cool, but sunny. As they entered the deprived area, Nancy felt as though she had stepped into the pages of *Tobacco Road*. Bill Frank's home was first on the list. Nancy's stomach did a flip as she saw the place. It was no more than a rotting, unpainted, three-room shack. As they walked through the front yard, it was necessary to step over rusting tin cans, pieces of old cars, feces (some of which Nancy suspected to be human), and the remains of several old cars. In addition, a skinny goat was nibbling on waist-high weeds.

The two teachers knocked on the front door, and a filthy child, who appeared to be about four years old and covered with the measles, opened the door and let them in. The room they entered was dark and had a terrible odor about it. It, too, contained pieces of rusted metal and parts of cars. A corner of the room was piled high with old clothing and dirty rags. Mrs. Datsun asked the child about this and was told, "That's where the kids sleep."

The back room contained a bed with sheets so dirty that they were brown. A month-old infant, who was also covered with the measles, lay screaming on the bed. An older baby, about one year old, was sleeping on the bed. To the right was the kitchen. The room was filled with dried, rotting food that looked and smelled months old. No clean dishes were in sight. The floor of the house was wooden with no rugs and was laden with soil and human filth.

They found Bill Frank's mother in the back yard washing clothes in a wooden tub. The water was so dirty it was black. Mrs. Parker was young, about twenty-five years old, slim, clean and rather attractive. With her was a half-naked little boy about two years old. He, too, had the measles, and was covered from head to foot with soil and feces. Traces of dried urine streaked down his legs. The only parts of him that were clean were his big, blue eyes. He handled his genitals, as he wore no pants, and then would put his fingers in his mouth. Bill Frank was sitting in the yard. He waved at his teachers, but made no move to approach them.

Mrs. Parker carried on a conversation easily. She explained that the water was dirty, because she had to haul it from the community well, and she only wanted to make one trip. She also spoke of how the authorities had threatened to take away her kids, if she did not clean up the house. This was the focus of her conversation. She was not interested in discussing Bill Frank or his problems.

Another one of the homes in which they visited was oddly shaped. Rather than being boxed-shaped, it was long and thin. Rooms had been added, one at a time, to the back. It, too, was in bad condition. Thirteen-year-old Kevin lived there. His mother was chopping wood in the front yard; so they were not invited inside. She told the teachers to "whup" Kevin whenever he needed it. She said he got whipped a lot at home, and she was certain he was bad at school. Mrs. Datsun assured the woman that Kevin was not bad. In fact, he was a good worker and never gave any trouble. The mother, however, still appeared skeptical.

Nancy felt depressed after the home visits. She had developed more compassion for the children, but was angry at a society that allowed this kind of poverty and ignorance to prevail. Knowing there was nothing she could do about the home-life, she decided to try and correct the injustice she was seeing in the school.

She talked with her college supervisor about the boys' not receiving free lunches for which they qualified. The college supervisor warned her not to do or say anymore about the situation. Puzzled, Nancy agreed. One week later, the principal announced to Mrs. Datsun that the punishment time was up and the boys could again receive school lunches. Much later, Nancy discovered that her supervisor had reported the situation to the state coordinator of special education. This person back-tracked down through the proper administrative channels, until the principal was forced by the superintendent to feed the youngsters.

Nancy encountered another problem that was not easily remedied. In a mainstreaming situation, it was imperative that regular and special class teachers keep the communication line open, reinforce each other's techniques, and keep the children on the appropriate instructional levels. This was accomplished in many instances, but there were two or three teachers in New Hampshire who insisted on ignoring the special needs of the children while they were in the regular classroom. Some even had the audacity to send in work from their classes, which was on levels too high for the children. They expected the special teacher to spend valuable time with this work rather than providing instruction at the proper levels.

Mrs. Datsun had tried to communicate with these teachers numerous times, but was unable to convince them of the necessity for their reinforcing each other. Consequently, these children were not profiting from special class placement.

Another memorable event for Nancy occurred when she was alone with the sixth grade boys. Several of them decided it was fun to slouch back in the seats, put their hands in their pockets and masturbate. Nancy tried to ignore this behavior at first, but when it became apparent that this was going to continue, she sent them outside to run around the school building several times. This seemed to stop the masturbating, at least for the "short haul."

As the end of the seven week period grew to an end, Nancy realized that she had much to learn. She had also discovered that she loved teaching and working with children. Seeing them grow and develop in even this short time provided compensation for the hard work and often frustrating times.

As a special treat for the children in the resource room, Nancy planned a thirty minute train ride and picnic at one of the state parks. They received permission slips and, surprisingly enough, money from the parents to pay for the train ticket. Even Bill Frank and Kevin came up with money to go. The children met in the resource room and then proceeded down the stairs to the waiting cars. Some of the mothers had offered to drive them to the train station. Nancy and Kevin were the last ones to leave the room, and being excited, Kevin was going down the stairs at a faster than usual speed. As he passed by the second floor, the principal reached out and grabbed the boy by the collar of his shirt. He took Kevin in this manner to his office. Nancy was surprised and curious. She followed them, staying a safe pace behind.

The principal took Kevin into his office, bent him over his desk, and proceeded to paddle him with a two-inch thick, hard, wooden board into which holes had been drilled. Nancy quietly watched from the hall as the boy was given about ten licks. Kevin never uttered a sound, but he was crying. Nancy began to shake uncontrollably and tears streamed down her face. She was fighting to resist an urge to attack the principal physically. When it was over, she gave the principal a hard glare, put an arm around Kevin's shoulders, and together they walked to the waiting cars. Kevin was quiet and withdrawn on the trip, and Nancy trembled for three days after the incident. This, too, she reported to her college supervisor.

Nancy's second seven week period proved to be much more pleasant. Her college supervisor had her placed in another school in a regular fourth grade classroom. The principal of this school was friendly and genuinely liked children. The supervising regular class teacher was the wife of the Baptist minister. She was young, and full of exciting ideas. She ran a democratic classroom and affection flowed between the teacher and her students. Nancy was welcomed into the room and allowed to try her methods.

Under Nancy's direction, the class studied a detailed unit on rockets, learned many folk dances, and took an enjoyable field trip to a bottling company. Nancy was also assigned to work with a nonreading boy in the class. A close relationship developed between the two of them and some reading success ensued.

Nancy felt that her student teaching experience had been excellent for her. She had seen two types of schools at close range, and discovered how important a principal could be in setting a school's atmosphere. The experience with both a resource room and regular classroom proved valuable in years to come. As a result of her student teaching, Nancy decided that she wanted to teach learning disabled children from lower incomes.

The next year she rejoiced in the news that the principal at New Hampshire School had not been rehired by that school system.

Stimulus Questions

1. What are the advantages of having experiences with both normal and handicapped students?
2. Other than interest centers in the classrooms, how can an older school building be made more attractive? How can this shabby appearance influence the learning that may go on?
3. What does "learning disabled" mean? Why do you suppose

most of the learning disabled children come from the poverty stricken area?

4. Do principals have the control to deny children free lunches? In what ways are they permitted to discipline students?

5. Where do you think Bill Frank should have been seated in the classroom? Why?

6. Was it a good idea to visit the homes, even after no response was heard from the notes? How else could contact with the parents have been made?

7. Were the teachers within their rights to enter the house when a parent or older person did not answer the door? What should they have done at this point?

8. How do you think Mrs. Parker felt when she saw the teachers coming out of her house?

9. Should the teachers have commented to Mrs. Parker about the filth and child neglect they saw? Why? Should this be reported, and if so, to whom?

10. Why do you suppose Bill Frank stayed away from the teachers?

11. Was the approach Nancy took to get the boys back their free lunches proper? What else could she have done?

12. Why is a strong line of communication between the special and regular class teachers necessary? Without this, what could happen to mainstreaming?

13. What are the benefits of field trips? What should be included in the preparations for one?

14. How should Nancy have reacted to the violent paddling she witnessed?

15. What is the principal's role in establishing a positive school climate?

16. In what ways did this student teaching experience prove valuable to Nancy?

VALLIE'S FITS

Highland Park Elementary School was located in a southern city of approximately 50,000 people. The majority of students came from middle-income families.

One of the kindergarten teachers at this school became ill and was unable to finish the last three months of the year. A middle-aged woman, Mrs. Warren, was hired as the replacement. She had taught three years after college before leaving the profession to raise her children. When this position became available, she was ready to return to teaching.

The new teacher was as excited as the children on her first morning at school. There were twenty-seven students in the class, and the room was buzzing with greetings and activity.

Vallie was the last child to enter the kindergarten room that morning. It was several minutes before Mrs. Warren noticed the child hugging the door frame. Vallie was quite small for her age, looking more like a baby than a little girl. She had matted, dirty, blonde hair that hung in strings around her face. Her bangs were so long, they almost covered her round, amber eyes. Her face and hands were covered with smudges. She was wearing a short-sleeve, tattered shirt with buttons missing. It was several sizes too large. Her torn blue jeans were rolled up at the bottoms and were kept up by an old, black cloth belt that was tied in a knot. Her feet were covered with dirty tennis shoes, again, several sizes too large, and she wore no socks. In spite of the cold weather, she had no coat or sweater.

As Mrs. Warren approached Vallie, she noticed a terrible odor, but in spite of it, she held out her hand. The child looked up at her with fear in her eyes, and she shrank back. The teacher smiled, waited, and finally, Vallie took Mrs. Warren's hand. The teacher told her her name, and as she led her into the classroom asked, "What's *your* name?." Before the child could answer, a tough looking little boy laughed and answered, "It's stinky Vallie... Old stinky Vallie has come to school." Mrs. Warren gave him a threatening look, and Vallie slipped silently into her seat at one of the large tables. She stared downward at her hands, as she gripped them together.

Not once during the day did the youngster interact with the other children. During free time she sat by herself and held onto a small, unclothed, baby doll. The other children didn't want the doll, for it had one eye punched out and an arm missing. At lunch Vallie ate every bite on her plate in nearly one gulp. It was as though she had missed several meals.

During naptime that day she had no blanket to lie on as did the other children. Vallie went to the closet and got out a couple of pieces of old newspapers, which she carefully spread out in a corner away from the other children. She was soon sound asleep.

Later, as the class was busy with work, Mrs. Warren heard a strange humming sound coming from Vallie. As she turned to walk in her direction the child fell out of her chair onto the floor. The muscles in her body contracted, and then her entire body shook and jerked. In a few seconds foam began to appear at her mouth. By that time all of the children in the class were staring, and before the seizure finished, many were crying, and one was screaming. Mrs. Warren was frantic and actually froze in her footsteps, saying over and over, "Oh, my God. Oh, my God."

Meanwhile, Vallie's shaking subsided, and she awoke with a confused look. Other teachers had entered the room, and the special education teacher, Mrs. Lee, recognized immediately that Vallie had had a grand mal seizure. She enlisted the aid of Mrs. Warren to help her carry the child to the bed in the nurse's office, where Vallie immediately fell into a deep sleep.

The nurse was not present that day, thus the two teachers had to change Vallie's clothes. During the seizure, the child had lost control of her bladder. She wore no underclothes, and as they took off her jeans, they found many welts and bruises. They both recognized this as a possible child abuse and neglect case, but they were afraid to get involved in this area. Both teachers agreed on saying nothing. They sponged her off and found some dry clothes in which to dress her.

Vallie awoke about the time school was out. Rather than sending her home on the bus, Mrs. Lee volunteered to drive her. Mrs. Lee hoped to talk with the child's parents about getting her to a doctor for tests.

Vallie was awake, but groggy; however, she was able to show Mrs. Lee the way to her home. To the teacher's surprise, it was not a house or apartment, but an old garage, which was barely visible from the street. It was located in back of another shabby looking dwelling. The opening in the garage for the car to enter was closed. Vallie led the teacher to a side door. Around the door lay several mangy dogs. They looked as though they had not eaten in days. Mrs. Lee and Vallie stepped over the animals and knocked on the door.

Presently, an unshaven, toothless, dirty man, who was wearing only overalls, opened the door. His age was indeterminate. He said nothing, but simply stood in the doorway. Mrs. Lee quickly explained who she was and what had happened to Vallie in school that day. With this explanation a disgusted look came on his face, and he snarled, "That kid's been having so many damn fits. Just bothers the rest of us. I know she's puttin' on. Wants attention. Don't you worry none. I'll stop them fits." Mrs. Lee answered, "I'm afraid you don't understand. You see, I believe Vallie can't help having them. That there may be some physical reason why they continue. I'd like to see her taken to the hospital for some tests." Vallie's father replied, "Ain't no kid of mine going to see no doctors. Ain't got no money no way. Forgit it." With those final words, he grabbed Vallie roughly by the shoulder, yanked her into the garage, and slammed the door.

Unwilling to take "no" for an answer, Mrs. Lee straightened herself up again, knocked on the door. When the door finally was opened, she stated, "Won't you please let me take Vallie to the hospital? It won't cost you a thing, and it might help her." As he was about to shut the door, a woman's voice from inside said, "Aw, let her go, Marvin, it can't do no harm. It'll be a good way to see if the kid is puttin' us on." To which the man replied, "Now just you shut up, woman. You ain't got no say in this, and you, teacher lady, get the hell out of here, before I sic them dogs on you." Mrs. Lee sighed, shook her head, and left.

The next day Vallie did not return to school. After another

week had passed, and still she had not appeared, both Mrs. Lee and Mrs. Warren became concerned. Mrs. Lee had discussed seizures with the kindergarten teacher. She had shown her how to react and take care of a person during and after an attack. Mrs. Warren passed this information on to the kindergarten children in order to prepare them for any future seizures they may witness. The children were almost eager for Vallie to return. They wanted to try out their newly gained knowledge.

Vallie was the oldest child in her family. There was no way to check on her absenteeism, except to return to the home. This time, both teachers visited, and to their relief, were greeted by Vallie's mother. The woman invited them into the garage, where they discovered that indeed, the family lived in one room. The floor was dirt, one window was covered with newspapers, and the place was heated by an oil heater, which was placed in the middle of the room. There were no chairs, only two mattresses and the back seat from an old car. These had been placed around the oil heater.

The three younger children were sitting quietly on the mattresses. They were filthy and covered with bruises. Vallie was sitting on the back seat, smiling shyly at the teachers. The teachers stood by the heater and discussed with the mother the importance of Vallie's having the tests. The mother agreed, and she signed papers giving permission for them to take the child for the examination. She promised to have her in school the next week.

On Monday morning Vallie arrived, filthy, but present. The teachers discussed cleaning her up, but decided to leave her in this condition for the hospital personnel to see. The nurses took one look and summoned social services. Fresh bruises and welts were discovered on the youngster's body. The social service representatives were so disturbed over what they saw that a judge was personally called in to see her.

X-rays were ordered in addition to an EEG. The irregular brain waves indicated definite epilepsy, but more interesting, was a hairline, skull fracture that the doctors agreed was the probable cause of the brain disturbance. This discovery led them to order further x-rays. To their dismay they discovered six earlier, untreated, fractures on various parts of her body. With this additional evidence, the judge ordered Vallie and the younger children to be placed under protective custody in a foster home. The state filed charges against the parents.

Vallie, at first, was bewildered by all of the attention she was receiving. She thoroughly enjoyed the bath and hair wash she received at the hospital. Mrs. Lee had talked with her earlier about what kind of clothes she liked the best, and the child answered, "Dresses, but I never had one." After the bath, Mrs. Lee was prepared with a new dress, underclothes, socks, shoes, and a coat. Vallie beamed as she saw herself in the mirror. Before she was taken to the foster home, the doctors provided her with medication to help control the seizures.

On the way to her new foster home, Vallie was asked what she wanted more than anything in the world, and she answered, "A doll." Naturally, a stop had to be made at a toy store, and a pretty baby doll was purchased for her. Vallie's eyes were sparkling as she cuddled the doll in her arms.

When she arrived, she found her younger brother and sisters receiving their baths and new clothes. They were quiet and withdrawn in the beginning, but within a week, they were laughing and playing with the new toys and each other. Not one of them asked about their parents.

When Vallie returned to school, with the seizures fairly well under control, she was hardly recognizable as the same child. The little boy, who had called her "stinky Vallie," stared at her for awhile, then said, "You sure do look nice, Vallie." Vallie smiled at him, then went over to play with her old friend, the one-eyed and one-armed doll.

Stimulus Questions

1. Why didn't Vallie's odor prevent Mrs. Warren from taking the child's hand? What else could the teacher have done?
2. Why do you suppose Vallie acted in fear of the new teacher.
3. What should Mrs. Warren have done about the nasty comments the little boy made to Vallie?
4. What could the kindergarten teacher have done to bring Vallie into play with the other children?
5. How do you suppose Vallie felt about having to take a nap on

the newspapers? Should the school provide mats for all children, if naptime is required? Why?

6. How do you suppose Mrs. Lee explained to the children about seizures?

7. How should teachers be prepared to handle the unexpected, such as a seizure? Should this be taught to teachers on college level or by the public schools?

8. What are a teacher's responsibilities by law when child abuse or neglect is suspected?

9. Whose responsibility was it to take Vallie home?

10. Whom do you suppose Mrs. Lee had in mind to pay for Vallie's tests when she told Vallie's father he wouldn't be responsible for the expenses?

11. What do you think about Mrs. Lee's persistence in the conversation with Vallie's father?

12. Was it proper for the teacher to check on Vallie's absenteeism?

13. Why did Social Service call in the judge?

14. What is the usual reaction of children towards their parents in child abuse or neglect cases?

CRYSTAL'S ATTACK

The fears and horrors of polio days were over. No longer did parents shudder with the thought of the long, hot summer days, when, like an ominous cloud, the disease hovered over their children. It had threatened not only their physical being, but their very existence. In many communities, public swimming pools, theaters, and parks were closed, and children were isolated in their homes and backyards. Then, in 1954 the Salk vaccine was a welcomed discovery. All over the country parents flocked with their children to physicians and health centers for the miracle, preventive drug. Thousands upon thousands of children were saved from being killed or maimed for life by this dreaded disease.

As the years passed, the public saw less and less of the effects of polio. Young parents learned about the disease only from second-hand information, and thus many became negligent about having their children vaccinated. Danny and Lena Crowe were parents who fell into this category. They were both from economically deprived homes, and neither had received any kind of preventive health care. They married early and began having children immediately. They did not realize the importance or the availability of immunizations for their children, and no one encouraged them in this area.

Danny Crowe dropped out of school at age sixteen, and although devoted to his family, did not have steady employment. When he did work, it was at odd maintenance jobs. Lena Crowe came from a large family and knew of no other choice for herself but having a family. When she married Danny at age sixteen, her goals were to have children. This was quickly accomplished. Crystal was the first child, then came Junior, Max, Louise, Candy, and Elvin. The children were all born in their small, wooden house. None had even been seen by a physician.

When Crystal entered the first grade, it was a requirement that all children have the necessary vaccinations. Danny and Lena took all the children to the health center that fall. It was then that their well-checks and immunizations were begun. The Crowe's were instructed to bring the children back in two months for the second administration of vaccines. They waited until March to do this. Since the immunizations were in progress, Crystal's school let her continue attending.

The following July, when Crystal was seven and one-half years old, Lena decided that it was time for her children to learn to swim. She took them to a cold, spring-fed pond near their house. The heat had been almost unbearable for them that summer, and the pond was a welcome relief.

Crystal had always been a happy, active child in spite of the family's low economic situation, but for several weeks, she had been listless and not interested in active play. She told her parents about drinking out of a stream, where later, she discovered a dead cat had been lying not far above her drinking spot. She became quite ill that night. They attributed her listlessness over the next few weeks to this incident.

One late afternoon the family went to the pond, and Crystal spent over an hour in the cold water. On the way home she began having chills. The next morning the child noticed her back was stiff when she leaned over to get her clothes. As the day progressed, Crystal began feeling worse and worse. By noon she was having chills and fever. Although the temperature was almost 100 degrees outside, Crystal wanted to be covered with all of the quilts they owned. That night she became delirious with the fever and was screaming about huge, black spiders crawling up the walls. This so alarmed the parents that they took the child to a physician the next morning. Upon examining her, the doctor diagnosed her condition as being a kidney infection and prescribed rest, lots of liquids, and sponge baths to break the fever.

On the third day Crystal's fever remained at 105 degrees, and she was still in and out of delirium. Again, the frightened parents took her to the doctor. This time the physician required her to walk across the floor, and sure enough, paralysis had begun to set in Crystal's left side. It had been a long time since the physician had seen a case of polio, but without hesitation, he gave the child a laxative. By doing so, he hoped to clear the intestinal tract of the germs, a practice which was seldom done and had no research basis for success. In this case, however, it may have helped.

Crystal was sent to a large hospital, approximately two hours away, which was equipped to perform an analysis of her spinal fluid. This was carried out the fourth day of the child's illness, and it confirmed that Crystal did have poliomyelitis. She was admitted to the hospital and kept in isolation. On the fifth day the fever subsided, and Crystal became alert. It was apparant the crisis was over.

Three more days passed and a spinal tap revealed an absence of the disease. Plans were then implemented to have Crystal transferred to a hospital for crippled children. The disease had left the child's entire left side quite weak, especially in the leg below the knee. She had tried to walk on several occassions, but her left knee had a tendency to buckle under her weight. Physical therapy was called for at this point in her recovery, and the Children's Hospital could provide this treatment.

Crystal was transferred to the other side of the city by ambulance. By now, the child was feeling fine, and other than the weak leg, she was as active as ever. The ride in the ambulance was a special treat. She bounded all over the back section, going from seat to bed, and then up front to talk with the driver. The ambulance attendants were puzzled as to why she was going to the hospital.

Danny and Lena were with Crystal on this day, and they were relieved to see her so active and feeling well again. They had been told, in detail, what to expect in the way of long-term recovery and treatment. Their main concern was how they would have transportation to visit the child. Social Services went into action and arranged for their transportation to and from the hospital every two weeks. Also, they were provided with a babysitter for the younger children on these days. Crystal also needed clothes. Their social service aide took care of this problem.

It was projected that Crystal would need therapy at the hospital from four to six months. No time was wasted in beginning her treatment. First, an analysis of the muscular weakness was made. Next, a plan for therapy was drawn up and initiated. This consisted of physical therapy in a warm pool, whirlpool baths, moist-heat for muscle relaxation, and a great deal of rest. The routine was regimented six days a week. Sundays were scheduled for rest and visitors.

Crystal was fitted with crutches and a short-leg brace on her left leg. The disease had left a particular impact on her foot. It had to be protected at all times. When the brace wasn't being worn, the foot was supported by a wooden box at the end of the bed, and sand bags were placed along the sides. As one might imagine, this limited the child's activity even in the bed. There was also concern about her spine becoming curved, as a result of muscular weakness in her back. Therefore, she was allowed to sit up in a wheelchair only thirty minutes three times a day. Walking and standing at the initial stage of therapy was totally forbidden.

As August progressed, it was soon time for Crystal to begin her academic studies. The local school system provided a special teacher for the children who were able to profit from instruction. Crystal fit this role. Mrs. Preston visited Crystal the third week in August to begin her tutoring session. Finding time for the lessons in between the therapy schedule was difficult, but at last, Mrs. Preston was able to work in an hour every morning. The teacher soon found Crystal to be a bright youngster, but one who was not in the least bit motivated to do work. The child simply would not do the day to day assignments, and it was impossible to cover all curriculum areas in the one hour time slot.

Mrs. Preston began to appeal to the nurses for help in encouraging the child to study. Again, this was difficult for them, as duty hours varied from week to week. Unable to think of another solution, Mrs. Preston decided to limit her instruction to reading, spelling, and arithmetic. She taught Crystal reading and spelling three times a week, and arithmetic the other two days. In spite of this schedule, Crystal began to fall behind her class.

The limiting activity was beginning to take a toll on the child's patience. Gradually, she began to get out of bed, unsupervised, and hop around the room on her good leg. A couple of times she tried swinging from the metal rod that held the curtain surrounding her bed. Her favorite activity was to climb on top of the seven foot wooden cabinets which held the clothes. Her physical therapist found her hopping around the room, and for punishment Crystal was deprived of her treasured "sitting up time." This punishment occurred quite often, and it was seldom that the child could take full advantage of the freedom and mobility which the wheelchair afforded.

When Crystal became more cautious about her extra physical activities, she turned to more subtle outlets. She had been given a set of perfume and powder. She and a friend mixed this all together and threw it at each other from bed to bed. She was in the middle of this when Mrs. Preston came for the tutoring session. Rather than calling a nurse, the teacher put a stop to the battle. She quickly cleaned up the mess and made the girls promise not to do this again. Mrs. Preston secretly felt that the restrictions placed on Crystal were not to her best advantage. She was seeing a slow personality change come over the child. In August the child was outgoing and friendly. In November she was becoming quiet and withdrawn except for an occasional incident like the perfume battle. The teaching sessions seemed to becoming talk or therapy sessions for the child. She and Mrs. Preston were developing a close relationship.

By the last of November, Crystal was back on her feet learning to walk again. Although it was with the assistance of the brace and crutches, she was happy to be out of bed, even during physical therapy. The doctors kept their earlier promise, and Crystal was allowed to return home before Christmas.

Home presented a whole new world of adjustment for the child. She was thrust into a small, crowded house, where she shared a bed with her two younger sisters. During her illness Crystal had become accustomed to having her own private bed. Lena and Danny tended to be overprotective with her which caused resentment among the other children. She received more than her share of attention from them.

School was another problem. The doctors were still concerned about Crystal's back and would only allow her to attend school three half days a week. With extra help from the teacher she was given assignments to do at home, but she continued to follow her pattern of not completing them. Lena was busy with the smaller children and wasn't interested in encouraging Crystal in this direction.

Mrs. Preston had developed such a fondness for the child that she traveled to Crystal's home twice a month to visit. The teacher and Lena also became good friends in the process. Concerned about the possibility of Crystal having to repeat the second grade, she contacted the superintendent about providing a home-bound teacher for Crystal. She reminded him about Public Law 94-142, and stated that she felt the child's needs were not being adequately met. After several discussions with him, the principal, and the teacher, it was decided that the school system could hire one of the substitute teachers to go to Crystal's home each afternoon and provide her with lessons. This was implemented, and by the end of the school it was decided that by attending the summer school sessions, Crystal would be ready for the third grade.

Although the child's academic needs had been met through the effort of Mrs. Preston, she had a long road ahead as far as her social and emotional life were concerned. Being from a low economic family compounded Crystal's problem. However, Mrs. Preston hoped that she could continue to work with the family, and assist Crystal to cope with the problems which lay ahead.

Stimulus Questions

1. What can be done to provide early health care for children?
2. Why were the Crowe's allowed to miss their second appointment to receive the vaccine? Who in the school was responsible for allowing the child to continue without the vaccination?
3. What are the cause and effect of poliomelitis? How may it be prevented?
4. What are some of the side effects of the disease?
5. Are children today totally protected against polio? Why is it necessary to continue to immunize children?
6. What could Mrs. Preston have done to encourage Crystal to study when the teacher was not present?
7. What could have been done about the scheduling difficulties?
8. What outlets could have been provided in the hospital for Crystal's energy?
9. How do you feel about her "sitting up" time being removed as a means of punishment?
10. How could the child have been prepared for the adjustment at home?
11. Was Mrs. Preston within her right to charge the school with not meeting the child's needs? Explain.

12. What do you feel was the most important thing Mrs. Preston provided Crystal? What problems did Mrs. Preston see ahead for Crystal?

OTIS! OTIS! OTIS!

Although school had been in session for two weeks, the
county system felt fortunate to hire Mrs. Humphrey as the
mental retardation resource room teacher even at this late date.
She had come to them with ten years of successful teaching
experience with handicapped children and excellent recommendations. Her assignment was to Slate Elementary School.

The special education coordinator was giving the new teacher
a tour of the county schools to familiarize her with the other
special education classes. As they entered Barnett School, Mrs.
Humphrey nearly ran into a boy who was wandering aimlessly
down the hall. Later, she saw him hanging upside down on the
metal banister going up the hall steps. The coordinator turned to
her and volunteered, "That's Otis Barnes."

Otis had been attending Barnett School for four years. According to his regular class teachers, he was uncontrollable. They
allowed him the freedom to roam around the school as he pleased.
He was always assigned to a room, but this wasn't enforced.
Often, the principal would paddle him for his wanderings, but
everyone knew it was just for the record. This never helped and
actually seemed to make matters worse. Otis was ten years old and
already written off by the school system as incorrigible.

A spark of hope was in the school, however. A new special
education class was being formed at Slate School. Otis's IQ score
had been too high for placement in the past, but on the third
attempt, his score fell at the cut-off point. The class at Barnett
happened to be full. Plans were quickly carried out to have Otis
transferred to Slate School. His placement committee decided
that the boy should be in a regular fourth grade class for
homeroom, recess, lunch, music and art, but receive four hours of

academic work in the class for educable mentally retarded children.

The special class structure was a cross between a self-contained room and a resource room. All of the fifteen children had schedules similar to Otis's in which they spend most of the day with Mrs. Humphrey. The children ranged in ages from nine to fourteen.

Fortunately, no one told Mrs. Humphrey about Otis's past school behavior; so she warmly accepted him into her class. In the beginning she wondered why he had been evaluated so many times, but after her informal assessment she discovered he was functioning at the second grade level. She then realized that he needed special academic help. He was very active but not to the distraction of the other students. Otis's communication skills were astounding. He could carry on an intelligent conversation with any adult.

In the class there were five boys, two sets of brothers and Otis, who became friends. Otis immediately became the leader. The boys looked up to him and followed his every whim. At first this didn't cause difficulty, but after a few weeks, dissension emerged. Mrs. Humphrey separated them into corners of the room. When questioned about the quarreling, the boys protected Otis as the source of the problem. "It's not Otis's fault," they would announce. In spite of the inner conflicts, Otis was staying in the classroom and not roaming in the halls as he had previously done. He was also functioning well with his normal class routine.

Other incidences began to crop up that disturbed Mrs. Humphrey. Ed was one of the boys in Otis's gang. He was from a poor and quite large family. His clothes were dirty and full of tears and rips. His pants often contained unsightly holes located at revealing places. One day, as Ed leaned over to turn off the record player, Otis began to laugh and point at Ed's behind. "He doesn't have on any underwear," jeered Otis, "and his ass is showing. Hey, look everybody." Ed turned around quickly while blushing, grabbed his pants together at the site of the hole, and slipped into his seat. By that time, the children in the room were also sniggering and laughing at Ed. Mrs. Humphrey intervened by announcing that it was time for reading, and she assigned all of them seatwork to do.

At recess Mrs. Humphrey asked Ed if he would like for her to mend his pants. He readily accepted her offer, and when it was done, he ran off to play. She called Otis in from outside and tried to talk with him about why he was teasing Ed. His only response was a sullen look and a glaring stare.

Another day, Otis entered the classroom dragging his feet and making a sharp scraping sound as he walked. Upon examining the bottom of his shoes, Mrs. Humphrey discovered that Otis had tacked bottle caps to the soles of his shoes. He reacted almost violently when he was asked to remove these caps. Mrs. Humphrey quietly explained that the caps were tearing up the wooden floors, and that they must be removed. "You old, God-damn bitch," yelled Otis. Mrs. Humphrey ignored his comment and gave him five minutes to remove the caps. Otis complied with her request.

Three buses arrived simultaneously each afternoon to take the special education children to their respective neighborhood schools for bus transfer. Mrs. Humphrey always stood by the door and called out each bus number. The children riding those particular buses filed out of the room and got on the bus.

Otis, whose bus was always the last to leave, slipped out the back door of the classroom just as the busses arrived. Mrs. Humphrey did not notice he was missing until the first two busses had pulled away. When all of the children riding the third bus had boarded, the teacher realized Otis was not among them. She stepped out of the classroom, and to her horror, she saw Otis hanging onto the side of the bus, trying to enter through a window. At that moment, the bus began to roll away. Mrs. Humphrey leaped over to the bus, grabbed Otis around the waist, and jerked him loose. This resulted in both of them falling backwards onto the rocky drive. By now the driver of the bus had stopped because of the cries of the children who were watching. Shaken, but uninjured, Mrs. Humphrey dragged Otis back into the classroom and proceeded to whack him twice with a board which had broken off the back of the desk. Shocked at being hit by Mrs. Humphrey, Otis became quite wide-eyed. He then got on the bus and left for home.

The paddling, even though not severe, was the force which ended any positive relationship between Otis and Mrs. Humphrey. Within a week Otis had caused three major fights, cursed Mrs. Humphrey on several occasions, and had entered the room with a switch-blade knife and threatened to "cut-up" anyone who bothered him. In addition, his hyperactivity was now distracting the other students. He was unable to cope with the regular class placement, thus he was assigned to Mrs. Humphrey on a full-time basis.

There was no counselor to whom Otis could be referred, and Mrs. Humphrey knew she must deal with the problem herself. She had had a successful home visit with Otis's mother at the beginning of the year. Now, she decided it was time to call the mother in for a conference. She was hoping to discover a reason for Otis's behavior, or enlist the aid of the mother in coping with the boy.

Mrs. Barnes had five children, lived in a small, unpainted farm house, and worked in a local sewing factory. She was the sole support of the family. Otis's father was reported to be a short, stocky, hot-tempered man who could not hold a job. He was presently serving a prison term for assaulting his last boss with a crow-bar. He had been in and out of prison many times during Otis's life.

Mrs. Barnes was able to leave the factory early enough to come in for a conference with Mrs. Humphrey after school. The woman said she had been up since 4:30 A.M. that morning working in the fall garden. She looked tired and haggard. Mrs. Barnes listened intently to Mrs. Humphrey, who described the difficulties Otis had been causing. The mother stated that as far as she knew, there was nothing happening at home to precipitate Otis's behavior. As a matter of fact, Mrs. Barnes said that this had been the best school year Otis ever had. She offered no suggestions, but said she would talk with him about his behavior. Mrs. Humphrey felt extremely frustrated after the conference. The teacher did remember to praise Otis's academic improvement to his mother.

Mrs. Humphrey received permission from Otis's mother to contact a physician about the child. She felt that medication to manage his hyperactive state might help the situation. With this permission in hand, Mrs. Humphrey proceeded to visit the Barnes's family physician. He listened intently, nodded, and wrote out a prescription. The doses were to be administered twice a day at school, once in the morning and once after lunch.

Otis was agreeable to taking the medication, but the effect was almost as bad as his hyperactivity. He became groggy and so irritable that it was difficult to tolerate his crankiness. Although he was in his seat more often than before, he constantly argued with Mrs. Humphrey and the other boys. Nothing pleased him, and his academic learning came to a complete halt.

Mrs. Humphrey made a telephone call to the physician to see if an adjustment in the doses should be made, and if so, how much. To her surprise, the physician gruffly said that there was nothing he could do and hung up on her. After talking with some of the other teachers at Slate School, Mrs. Humphrey learned that the physician, himself, had a handicapped son who was severely retarded, hyperactive, and unable to attend school. Mrs. Humphrey assumed that this case was a sensitive area with the man and that he was unable to cope with a situation so similar to his own.

Realizing that she had no alternative, Mrs. Humphrey began adjusting the dose herself. She gave Otis smaller amounts more frequently, but at the same time, did not exceed the initial recommended dosage. Some improvement was noticed in Otis's mood, but it was obvious that medication was not the answer.

Otis did not appear in class one morning. Since he had never been absent, Mrs. Humphrey found herself looking forward to a day without the child's disruptions. But about ten o'clock, in walked Otis. Mrs. Humphrey sighed inwardly but tried to smile pleasantly at him. He explained his absence by telling about missing the bus at Barnett School. The boy had actually walked five miles to come to Slate School that day. Feeling somewhat guilty at being happy about his absence, Mrs. Humphrey put her arm around his shoulder and gave him a little squeeze. Otis beamed for the first time that year.

One cold, bitter day Otis staggered in the classroom. His eyes were glazed, and he was clutching his left arm. He sat quietly in his seat and stared off into space. When Mrs. Humphrey asked him what was wrong, he stated that he had fallen against the stove and burned his arm. She looked at his arm, and indeed, there was a nasty burn. When asked how he had fallen, he said that his sister had thrown a frying pan at him and in trying to dodge it, he had fallen against the hot stove. The school nurse took care of the wound, and Otis slept on a mat the remainder of the school day.

Mrs. Humphrey found out later that Otis's father had just gotten out of prison. He had a reputation of beating his children when he first came home, and Mrs. Humphrey suspected that the burn had been the work of an angry father and not a sibling fight. The teacher did not know how to go about proving this was the case, but she was on the alert for any other physical problem with Otis that may be linked to abuse. There were none other during the year.

Mrs. Humphrey stayed in the community three years, and taught Otis two more years. He progressed well academically; but emotionally, there was little improvement. She heard several years later that Otis was serving a jail term for stealing cars.

Stimulus Questions

1. How could Otis's behavior have been managed better when he was in the regular classroom?
2. What criteria other than IQ tests should be examined before placing a child in a special education class? Do you think this was the best placement for Otis? What would be alternative placements?
3. Why was it fortunate that no one told Mrs. Humphrey about Otis's past record?
4. What leadership qualities did you see in Otis? How could Mrs. Humphrey have used these qualities to the best advantage?
5. How well do you think Mrs. Humphrey handled Otis's teasing Ed? What else could she have done?
6. Should teachers ignore profane language in the classroom? Why?
7. Was Mrs. Humphrey right to have paddled Otis? Why did it end the chance for a positive relationship?
8. What could she have done to manage his aggressive behavior?
9. Do you think Mr. Barnes's trouble with the law influenced the boy's behavior? How?
10. How do you think Mrs. Barnes felt about the discussion with Mrs. Humphrey? What should be included in parent conference?
11. Should physicians give medication for hyperactivity over the

phone? Should it be given at all? Why?

12. Should Mrs. Humphrey have contacted another physician? Do you think it would have helped? Why?

13. Do you think Otis knew how Mrs. Humphrey felt about him? How?

14. What should Mrs. Humphrey have done about the suspected child abuse?

15. Identify Otis's problems. What are his strengths?

A TOUCH OF LOVE

As Mrs. Fair drove along the bumpy road, she wondered what Rosa's new house would be like. The girl's family moved so frequently that it was difficult to keep up with them. As Rosa's first teacher, Mrs. Fair never let herself loose track of the family, even when they moved to other districts. The youngster had been absent from school for a week, and Mrs. Fair felt a strong urge to check on the reason. Also, she had not made a home visit since this latest move.

Mrs. Fair first met eight-year-old Rosa two years ago when the child entered her class for educable mentally retarded children. In addition to the retardation, Rosa was suffering from muscular dystrophy, which not only caused fat to be substituted for muscle tissue, but it was a terminal disease. At this time, Rosa was walking with the aid of crutches. Although the child had been classified academically at the educable level, her language development was excellent, and she was quite verbal. That, plus her sunny disposition, led Mrs. Fair to develop a strong attachment to Rosa. The child was a delight. She always had a smile and kind word for the teachers and students in school.

Twice that first year Rosa left the class as her family moved around the area. This pattern of moving also continued the second year. As Rosa began her third year in school, the muscular dystrophy had progressed to the point that she had to be placed in a wheelchair. Her legs were no longer strong enough to hold her body weight, even with crutches. On the positive side, however, Rosa still had good use of her upper extremities for both gross and fine motor control. Mrs. Fair was pleased that although Rosa's legs were not functioning, she still had bladder and bowel control. She continued to be a sweet, happy child.

106

Mrs. Fair sighed aloud as she located Rosa's "new" residence. The house was located beside the highway on the edge of a field that was typical for the rural, Southern region. The boards of the three-room house were gray and weather-beaten. Many were hanging loosely from the frame. The entire structure leaned noticeably to the left. Five rotting boards led up to the sagging porch. Tattered blankets were thrown across the one remaining railing. The house rested on footings made of rocks. These were widely separated underneath the house to allow for air movement during the hot summer months, but afforded no insulation against the cold in the winter. The roof was tin, which had rusted over the years. Some of the windows still contained panes, but most were covered with plastic.

The yard was only dirt and rocks and two, small, gnarled windblown trees stood side by side in one corner. There were several shells of old dilapidated cars also on the property. One could see an outhouse in the back. A bath tub was in sight in the side yard.

Mrs. Fair climbed the steps to the porch cautiously, for it, too, sagged beneath her weight. The house seemed unusually quiet, for Rosa had eight brothers and sisters, all under fourteen years of age. On previous visits Mrs. Fair had seen children everywhere, but today, none were to be seen or heard.

The teacher knocked on the door frame and waited for an answer. None came. She knocked again, with the same results. As she turned to leave, she was stopped by what she believed to be a slight moan. She listened quietly, and presently, a stronger sound came from within the house.

Without hesitation, she opened the door, and to her horror, she discovered Rosa lying face down on the floor. The child was so weak she could not lift her head. It was apparent to Mrs. Fair that the child had been in this same position for several days. As she looked around the room for something warm to put around Rosa, she saw that it was entirely empty. Everything was gone. Remembering the quilt on the railing outside, she got it quickly and wrapped Rosa snuggly in it. With difficulty, she then picked up the youngster and carried her to the car. Rosa had, again, slipped into unconsciousness. Mrs. Fair drove at maximum speed to the nearest hospital.

A physician on duty checked Rosa over carefully and diagnosed severe dehydration, malnutrition, and pneumonia. Fluids, nourishment, antibiotics, and warmth were administered during the night, and the next morning the child awoke exhausted but alert.

Mrs. Fair had not left her bedside all night. She was there the moment Rosa opened her eyes. "Rosa," said Mrs. Fair, "what happened to you?" Rosa bit her lower lip and cast her eyes downward. "Mama got sick and died last week," stated the youngster. "Daddy said he didn't want no crippled kid who was going to die too; so he took the other kids and left me. I tried to follow them, but my legs wouldn't go."

By this time tears were streaming down Rosa's cheeks, and she was in Mrs. Fair's comforting arms. The teacher promised that she would remain with her that day, leaving only to call the school to notify them of the situation and to request a substitute teacher for her class. She also went home for a shower and clean change of clothes.

In the meantime, the police were searching for Rosa's father on the charges of child neglect and attempted murder. A judge declared Rosa a ward of the state and social services began searching for a suitable foster home for the child. For the present, however, she would remain in the hospital.

Mrs. Fair was true to her word and sat with Rosa all day. That night, however, she felt a responsibility to go home and stay with her husband and children. Rosa seemed to be doing better and had spent a comfortable day. About ten o'clock that night, Rosa was having a conversation with Mrs. Leon, the head nurse, when the child lapsed into a coma. The hospital personnel worked in vain to bring her back to consciousness. Mrs. Fair rushed to the hospital the next morning when she was notified of Rosa's condition, but she could do nothing but wait. She returned to class three days after having discovered the abandoned child.

After a long week, Rosa finally resumed consciousness, but she was weaker than ever. The muscular dystrophy was moving at an alarming rate, taking the muscles of her body as it progressed. In spite of her weakness, she still displayed a cheerful outlook.

The nurses in the hospital quickly became attached to Rosa, that is all except Mrs. Leon. The nurse had made a promise to herself that she would never become involved with any of her patients. She felt that this did the patients no good and would only drain herself of needed energy. For fifteen years she had lived by this philosophy. She was an excellent nurse who performed her job in an efficient, businesslike manner.

Seeing that Rosa had no family, many of the nurses took it upon themselves to bring her flowers and toys. Mrs. Fair also came by every day. She had brought the youngster a soft, frilly, pink gown and bathrobe and Rosa wore them all the time.

Rosa was a talkative child and would make conversation with all of the nurses, even Mrs. Leon. Gradually, Mrs. Leon began staying with the child longer and longer. After three weeks she, too, had been mesmerized by Rosa. Mrs. Leon found herself looking forward to going to work in order to see her. One day this nurse came in with a cuddly, white bunny that had light brown spots on its body. A big pink bow was tied around its neck. Rosa squealed with delight when she saw the present. "Oh, Bunny," she said. "I've been waiting for you for so long." She took the bunny and hugged it to her chest. This pleased Mrs. Leon immensely, and from then on she and Rosa were best of friends.

Mrs. Fair had the children at school to make Rosa drawings and other art works. They also kept a continuous supply of cards and letters coming to her, both from her class and from other children in the school. Mrs. Fair also came by to see her each afternoon and spent some time helping her with school work. Many days, however, Rosa seemed too tired to manage much work.

The police finally discovered Rosa's father living in an abandoned warehouse in a nearby county. He had left the other children with relatives and was spending his welfare check on alcohol. He was arrested and charged with child neglect and attempted homicide. The children were all located and either stayed where they were or were placed in foster homes. Rosa was too ill to be removed from the hospital.

Rosa's condition steadily disintegrated. She became weaker every day, until she could not move herself at all. Through it all, she was still happy and smiling. The nurses actually fought over her care, and Mrs. Leon even came to see her on her off hours. Again, Rosa contracted pneumonia. She was given medicine, oxygen, lifesaving fluids, but none were effective. Exactly four months to the date of her arrival, Rosa died.

The entire hospital staff was in mourning as were the children and teachers who knew her. Mrs. Fair came by the empty hospital room to dispose of the youngster's things. While she was packing, Mrs. Leon entered the room and said to Mrs. Fair, "I want you to know how much Rosa meant to my life. I was a selfish, self-centered person until I met Rosa. That child has shown me how to love again." Mrs. Fair answered with, "Rosa touched all of our lives in her eight short years." With that, she smiled and handed the bunny to Mrs. Leon.

Stimulus Questions

1. Why do you think Mrs. Fair was so attached to Rosa? Why did she feel compelled to keep up with the family's whereabouts?
2. In addition to the description in the story, what are some other facts about muscular dystrophy? What is the usual prognosis?
3. Would Rosa have been allowed to continue in public school if her bowels and bladder had failed? What would be the alternatives for placement?
4. How do you think Mrs. Fair felt when she discovered Rosa abandoned in the house? Did she react to the best advantage?
5. How do you think the school system reacted when Mrs. Fair called in and said that she would be staying with Rosa? Should she have remained with the child?
6. Why do you think the disease was progressing at such a rapid rate?
7. Do you agree with Mrs. Leon's philosophy of not becoming involved with patients? Why?
8. Why is it a good idea for a child in the hospital to keep in contact with classmates? What are some other ways this may be accomplished?
9. What do you think "triggered" Rosa's father to abandon her? Do you think he was a "fit" father? Should he ever be allowed to regain custody of his other children? Why?
10. Should Rosa have been taken away from her family earlier? Why?
11. How can teachers prepare students for a classmate's death? What attitude about the child should be taken after death occurs?

THE OUTCASTS

In class, everyone avoided sitting behind Herschel when they could. It wasn't that his body odor was so bad, but he reeked of stale tobacco and snuff. Often in the classroom he would put snuff into his mouth, spit into his hand, and rub it off in his pockets. After a few hours, the smell permeated the area around him. The other students were relieved when Herschel would break a bone and have to remain at home. They didn't understand the seriousness of his illness.

Herschel had osteogenesis imperfecta, a condition in which bones are extremely brittle, and thus, are broken easily. Herschel was out of school much of the time in his younger years, but at age fourteen, the breaks were becoming less and less frequent. This improvement often occurs as youngsters enter puberty.

This medical problem had weakened the boy's body. Herschel was small, thin, and frail looking. In addition he had poor vision and was required to wear thick lenses in his glasses, which had been provided for him by the health department. His entire wardrobe consisted of two longsleeve, plaid shirts, two pairs of baggy, khaki pants, and one pair of ankle-high tennis shoes. The tobacco stain was permanently displayed around the side of his pants where he wiped his hands.

Throughout his school history, Herschel had attended a regular class. When he broke an arm or leg and had to remain at home in casts, a visiting teacher came to his house. In this manner, he kept up with his class. Indeed, this was not difficult, for Herschel was a highly intelligent boy. He learned quickly and received A's with little or no effort, in spite of the fact that he missed a good deal of school.

Herschel had one friend, named Eugene. Eugene was not as

bright as Herschel, but he did well in school. This was due mainly to the fact that Herschel spent much of his time tutoring Eugene. The two boys were a strange sight together. While Herschel was small and weak, Eugene was quite large and overweight. He ate constantly and even smuggled food into his classes. When Herschel was at home waiting for one of his bones to heal, Eugene ate even more.

Herschel's father was a truck driver who was absent from home much of the time. Although he made a decent salary, his family saw little of the money. He spent it on gambling and women he met on the road. He was a large, strong man who had no use for weaklings. Unfortunately, he felt Herschel was in this category. Mr. Evans totally ignored the boy when he was at home. He was not the least impressed with Herschel's academic skills. On one occasion he even sneered at one of his son's report cards and called him a "sissy."

Mrs. Evans, Herschel's mother, was a small, frail woman who had borne six children. Two died soon after their birth. She worked at a local shoe manufacturing company to help feed the children. Her job was to cut strings off the bottom portion of the shoe before soles were attached.

The oldest son, Monty, was eighteen years old. Monty was built like his father and had not been a successful student. He had been in and out of trouble with the law for years. His mother had no control over his activities. He did not live at home, but came and went as his finances dictated. Herschel was the next child, then came Louella, Fred, and Berta.

Because of Herschel's illness his mother assumed an overprotective stance toward the boy. She waited on him hand and foot and bragged about his academic accomplishments to the other children. Her attitude caused them to build up a resentment against Herschel. Monty was particularly affected and took out his jealousy by physically attacking his younger brother. Many of Herschel's broken bones were due to Monty's aggressive behavior toward him. Herschel lived in constant fear of these attacks. Monty had sworn to kill him if he told anyone.

Herschel had never had a teacher in his school career with whom he could identify, until he had Mr. Mackey for ninth grade science. Mr. Mackey realized the boy's potential ability and worked hard praising and encouraging Herschel. He had over-heard a conversation between Herschel and Eugene about how they planned to quit school at age sixteen, get jobs, and buy cars. Mr. Mackey was determined not to lose either one of them. The teacher even stayed after school many days to help them with a special science demonstration, which he had encouraged. He wanted them to enter it in a regional science contest. The boys held Mr. Mackey in high regard and put forth effort to please him.

Herschel and Eugene had always been the brunt of jokes around the school. Such terms as "four eyes," "scarecrow," "fatso," and "queer" were frequently bestowed upon them. Since neither of them was physically able to participate in sports, they were left out of the social functions. Herschel's odor didn't help matters. No one understood how Eugene could stand to be around him, but he continued to be a faithful friend.

One afternoon after school Herschel arrived at home to be greeted by Monty. The younger children were outside playing. His parents were gone so Herschel was alone with Monty. The older boy had been drinking heavily, and Herschel knew he was in for another beating. He was in for a surprise. Monty locked the doors and sexually assaulted him.

Herschel was terrified and retreated into silence. Mrs. Evans was the first to notice the change in Herschel, but she couldn't get him to tell her anything. He began waking up at night screaming, but, still, he would not tell anyone about the incident.

Mr. Mackey and Eugene were quite concerned about the change in Herschel. He had always been a quiet boy, but in his present state, he was totally withdrawn from them. He refused to help Eugene with schoolwork, so both of their grades dropped dramatically. He showed no interest in the science project and even began missing days at school. He refused to communicate with anyone.

A month later the family received word that Monty had been killed. He had gotten into a fight at a local tavern and had pulled a knife on a man who had just been released from prison for attempted murder. Herschel was relieved to know that the attacks had come to an end, but he was still having difficulty coping with the memory of the experience.

Herschel had always loved animals, especially cats. He was

continually bringing strays home and wanting to keep them, but his mother limited the number he could have to two. Big Boy was his favorite. Herschel found him when he was a kitten and had had him for five years.

Herschel was sitting on the steps of his porch one day watching workmen dig a large trench next door, when he saw a huge dog chase Big Boy into a corner of the house. The dog was angry and looked as though he was ready to kill the cat. Herschel jumped up from his seat and ran in the direction of his cat. In his haste to reach it, he tripped over some of the workmen's equipment and fell several feet into the ditch. The workmen came running to check on him and discovered him to be knocked out. One man saved Big Boy from the dog, and another went to call an ambulance.

Upon his arrival at the hospital it was discovered that Herschel had severe breaks in both legs and one arm. This time the doctors required that Herschel be sent to an orthopedic hospital in a nearby city rather than be sent home with the casts. He needed to be in traction that could only be provided in a hospital setting.

This had happened a couple of times before, so Herschel was not upset by the idea. As a matter of fact, he was happy not to have to continue with school and the pressures of Eugene and Mr. Mackey wanting to know what was wrong. He would receive tutoring in the hospital and keep up with his ninth grade work. The only things he missed were his snuff, smoking, and his cat.

Eugene was able to come to visit him several times during the two months' stay in the hospital. Herschel was always glad to see him, for Eugene would smuggle in snuff. Mr. Mackey also came to visit. Because of his mother's job, she was able to see him only on Sundays. Mr. Evans never came, but then, Herschel did not expect him.

After the breaks had healed, Herschel was allowed to return home with long-leg braces to protect against further injury. This was the worst part, for Herschel hated the heavy, restricting metal braces. He was coming out of his depression, though, and things were slowly returning to normal.

During a science period, soon after Herschel's return to school, another boy got upset because Herschel was sitting where he wanted to be. The boy put his hands on Herschel's shoulders and told him to move. Herschel exploded in a rage, screaming "Get your hands off of me. Don't you ever touch me." He then fell into uncontrollable sobbing. Mr. Mackey went over to Herschel and attempted to calm him down by talking gently to him. He dismissed the other students who were standing around watching.

When Herschel became calm, Mr. Mackey encouraged him to talk. It was then the truth was revealed. Herschel told Mr. Mackey about the earlier beatings and, finally, the sexual assault he had received from his older brother. Since the brother was no longer a threat, Mr. Mackey did not feel the necessity of telling anyone about the incidents. He simply assured Herschel that he would be available to listen whenever he felt like talking.

After this outpouring, Herschel's grades began to improve until they were back to their usual height. He began helping Eugene again. There was no more talk of dropping out of school at age sixteen. Also Mr. Mackey was able to convince Herschel to stop dipping snuff. This improved his odor tremendously.

This session of broken bones was the last for Herschel. He continued to wear the brace for several months, but by the time school started in the fall, he was free of them.

Herschel did not attend college, but with Mr. Mackey's assistance, he did go to a local two-year technical school where he graduated with honors.

Stimulus Questions

1. Tell what you know about osteogensis imperfecta. Describe what causes the condition, how it affects the body, and the usual outcome.
2. What is the role and function of a visiting teacher? What kind of children does he or she usually serve?
3. In what range do you suspect Herschel's intelligence to be? Is this level in any way related to his physical condition?
4. What do Herschel and Eugene have in common? Why are they friends?
5. How did Herschel's father influence his life? Could anything have been done to change Mr. Evan's opinion of Herschel?
6. Why was Mrs. Evans overprotective with Herschel? Was this an asset or liability to him?

7. How did Monty get away with beating Herschel all these years, particularily when Mrs. Evans was so cautious with the boy? Why didn't she suspect anything?

8. What do you think Mr. Mackey saw in Herschel that made him realize the boy's potential ability? What other things could he have done to encourage the boys to stay in school?

9. What can teachers do about children whom they suspect of being sexually molested? What are some of the signs to look for in the youngsters?

10. Why didn't Herschel tell anyone about Monty's attack on him, even after Monty's death?

11. How do you think Mr. Mackey handled Herchel's outburst in the classroom?

12. Was Mr. Mackey right in not telling anyone about the assault on Herschel? Explain. What should he have done if the brother has been living and remained a threat to Herschel?

13. What was Mr. Mackey's influence on Herschel's life?

TOBY'S WORLD

The city's low rent housing complex was designed so that five apartments shared one small yard. In the back yard were clotheslines, which on nice days were filled with drying clothes. Most of the apartments contained two bedrooms, although there were a few three bedroom ones available. As usual in this type of arrangement, the lists were filled with families waiting for a vacancy to occur.

Ten-year-old Toby Bryson shared a bedroom with his thirteen-year-old sister. Their mother had the other room to herself. An older sister was married to an engineer, whom she had met while he was in school at the nearby university. Mr. Bryson had not lived with the family in five years.

The financial situation of the family was not good. Mrs. Bryson worked at the local laundry to support herself and the two children. They received no assistance from her husband, older daughter, or the government. Toby's mother worked long, hard hours at the laundry to make ends meet.

The housing development afforded the family the opportunity to keep warm and clean, but they ate many meals of warmed-over beans, cornbread, and peanut butter. They had none of the minor luxuries of life, except for an old, battered television, which worked occasionally. They didn't own a car, so Mrs. Bryson was dependent upon neighbors for her transportation to work.

Toby had been a quiet baby who seldom cried. He ate well, slept well, and was little or no trouble. Mrs. Bryson took him to the health clinic for his check-ups and vaccinations. When Toby was two-and-a-half years old, Mrs. Bryson began to wonder about his quietness and lack of speech. He was a happy, lovable child; so she dismissed it with "he'll come along."

When a year later Toby still had no speech, the Health Department referred him to a pediatrician. After checking the child's hearing the pediatrician sent Toby to an eye, ears, nose, and throat specialist. Here, it was discovered that Toby was extremely hard-of-hearing. The specialist recommended that Toby be sent to a residential school for deaf and hard-of-hearing children. Mrs. Bryson was shocked, and refused to even consider that route. She decided to take him home and do the best she could for him.

It was about this time that Mrs. Bryson began working at the laundry. Since Mr. Bryson was still at home and did not have a job, three-year-old Toby was left in his care. Toby's sisters were in school most of the day. Mr. Bryson stayed drunk the majority of the time while Toby wandered around the apartment. Finally, when Toby was almost five, his father left the family permanently after a disagreement with his wife.

After the marriage dissolution, Toby began staying with a neighbor who took care of his basic needs but seldom gave him any attention. Thus, by the time Toby was of school age he had received little in the the way of readiness or stimulation.

Upon entering school Toby was placed in the first grade. An attempt was made to evaluate his ability, but the best IQ they could derive was a score of 60. This information, along with the fact that he was hard-of-hearing, led the placement committee to assign him to the resource room for educable mentally retarded children. This was the only special class the school had to offer. He attended this class for most of the day. Unfortunately, the special teacher had no training in working with deaf children. Again, Toby spent day after day receiving no instruction.

Toby was a good child. He sat at his desk and looked at picture books or played with games or toys. He smiled and laughed frequently with the other children. He was accepted quite well and was always included in the games at recess. He was especially skilled at any type of ball activities.

His undemanding behavior made it easier for the teacher to overlook him and his lessons. The only problem that was noted with the child stemmed from his adverse reaction to adult males. The only male in the school was the principal, and when he entered the classroom or approached Toby's group, the boy would begin screaming in his deep voice and hide himself behind the teacher or run to the restroom. The principal was kind and understanding. He did not try to force himself on Toby, but nothing was being done to help Toby overcome his fear.

Toby had been promoted from grade to grade with the same group of children each year. His fourth year in school a new coordinator of special education was hired for the county. She took an immediate interest in Toby. She borrowed a hearing amplifier and tried it with the youngster. It was apparent that he did have some hearing, for when he was put on the machine he listened intently to the noise in the room. After about ten minutes, however, he removed the earphones, obviously annoyed with what he was hearing. The coordinator realized that this was not the key to reach him.

The coordinator did put pressure on his teacher to present him with academic work each day. Soon, he began to learn to read nouns and verbs by associating the written word with an object or an action, such as a picture of a boat with the word, boat, written beneath the picture. He seemed to understand, and soon he was pointing out his new words in books and finding objects and pictures to match.

Toby's communication system up to this period had consisted of pointing, grunting, and a special sign language he had developed. The coordinator knew American Sign Language. She began to work with Toby each day on the proper signals. Again, he acquired these easily and quickly.

The coordinator was encouraged by his progress, and she visited with Mrs. Bryson to encourage her to send Toby to a residential school for the deaf. The mother was more receptive to the idea than she had been earlier, but was not financially able to consider the idea. The coordinator agreed to help her find support for Toby's schooling.

A crisis occurred in midyear when the principal found Toby and another fourth grader in the hall without permission. They had gone to the lunchroom to get extra milk. The principal sent them back to their classroom, but Toby responded to him by becoming hysterical. The principal was unable to calm him down. He picked him up, threw Toby over his shoulder, and carried him, screaming and kicking to the special teacher. He did relax when the principal left, but sat trembling with his head on his desk the remainder of the day.

When the coordinator heard about the incident she paid Mrs. Bryson another visit. Toby's problem had to be solved, before he could be sent to a special school. With much reluctance Mrs. Bryson related what she thought had caused Toby's fear.

When Toby's father had heard the news about his son's hearing difficulty, he was extremely upset. From that time on he reacted negatively to the boy. He was all for sending him to an institution, but the mother refused. This had been the source of many of their disagreements.

One day while Mr. Bryson was keeping Toby, Mrs. Bryson came home early from work. She discovered Toby tied to a clothesline in the back. As it turned out, the father had been keeping the child there each day for two weeks after the mother left for work. He would untie him an hour before she returned home. Mrs. Bryson noticed that Toby had been unusually possessive of her, but she had no idea why this was happening. A call to her from one of the neighbors alerted her to the situation, so she came home to see it for herself.

Fortunately, it was in the spring time; the weather had been pleasant so the child had not suffered from exposure. Mrs. Bryson ordered her husband out of the apartment. That was when the marriage break-up occurred. From that time on, Toby had reacted violently to men. The coordinator realized that this problem must be dealt with immediately.

Stimulus Questions

1. Why did the health department not notice Toby's lack of normal speech development?
2. Is the only answer for hearing impaired children a residential school?
3. How do you think Mrs. Bryson feels about such residential schools?
4. Was placement in the EMR classroom appropriate for a hard-of-hearing child? By law, what is the school system required to do about a child such as Toby?
5. How can a teacher with no formal training in working with deaf children deal with a child like Toby?

6. What should have been done when Toby's fear of adult males was first observed?

7. Was it important that Toby be promoted with the same group of children each year? How could this help or hurt him?

8. Would a residential school be good for Toby after his four years of school experience in the public school?

9. How else could the principal have handled Toby's fear in the hallway other than using physical force?

10. What do you think can be done to help Toby get over his fear of men?

11. Why do you think Mrs. Bryson was reluctant to tell the coordinator about the incident with Toby's father?

12. What should be the coordinator's next steps concerning Toby?

THE HIDDEN CURRICULUM

W hen they entered the fifth grade classroom at the beginning of school, Mervin and Grady Shackleford were unusually quiet, but as they became familiar with their new room and teacher, they began to communicate more openly. The teacher's aide, Mrs. Bennett, had a difficult time trying to understand them. They called her, "Mi' Benny."

Mrs. Bennett was a woman approximately forty-eight years of age. After completing three years of college, she dropped out to get married with all intentions of returning to complete her degree. She became pregnant shortly after her marriage, and her return to school was delayed by this child. Three more soon followed. The thoughts of returning to college lingered in the back of her mind, but the task of raising four children depleated her energy and ambition. This year Mrs. Bennett felt she was ready to expand her life. Three of her children were now living away from home. When the position of teacher's aide became available, she applied and was given the position.

There were thirty youngsters in the fifth grade class, including Mervin and Grady. The lead teacher was Miss Cambell, a young woman who was in her second year of teaching. On the surface the two women got along well together, but actually, Miss Cambell was unsure how to best use Mrs. Bennett's services. In addition, the younger woman felt somewhat threatened by the presence of an older person in her classroom. Regardless of these feelings, Miss Cambell had herself an aide. She was determined to make the situation a pleasant one for them both.

Mrs. Bennett on the other hand, felt sure of herself as an aide. She respected the younger woman and followed her orders cheerfully. The main concern was for Mervin and Grady. Both boys had repeated grades and were presently receiving help with part of their work from the resource room teacher and a speech therapist. They were reading only on the primer level, and their math skills were not a great deal higher.

Physically, Mervin and Grady were about the size of the normal ten and eleven-year-old boys in the class. Twelve-year-old Grady was a handsome child. He was blonde, had crystal blue eyes, straight white teeth, and soft features. Mervin, who was thirteen, was not so attractive. This older boy had mousy, brown hair, small, grey-brown eyes, rotting teeth, and coarse features. Although Grady was the younger brother, he was at least a half-a-head taller than Mervin. Both boys were disturbingly thin and undernourished.

The fifth grade classroom was one of the smaller ones in the school. In fact, it was located in a trailer. The windows were on the east side facing the main school building. They allowed for little or no fresh air to blow into the room. One door on the west side provided the only source of true ventilation in the room. When the door was open, flies, bees, and other flying insects would enter the room and disturb the children as well as the teacher.

Mervin and Grady had not had good baths for quite a long time. This fact was proven by their stifling body odor. They wore rags for clothing, and these had not been washed for weeks. The combination of this unbearable smell, the heat of the August days, and the lack of ventilation made the school room unpleasant. When the door was open, the boys would attempt to "flip" the flies with rubber bands, or the girls would squeal and scream as the bees buzzed around their heads. When the door remained closed, the youngsters complained bitterly about the nauseating smell. These initial days were, indeed, long and hard to bear.

After a couple of weeks, Mrs. Bennett took it upon herself to gather information about the Shackleford family. This was obtained through school records, discussions with other teachers, and residents of the town. The aide discovered that the family consisted of both parents and ten children. Mervin and Grady were born somewhere in the middle. After the birth of the tenth baby, the family physician convinced Mrs. Shackleford to have a tubal ligation. The last child was presently two years old. Mr. Shackleford did not have a steady job, but he occasionally picked tobacco for extra income in the summer.

In the meantime the situation in the room was becoming critical. The other fifth graders began taunting, teasing, and even threatening fights with "stinky ol' Mervin and Grady." It was obvious that a solution had to be found quickly.

Mrs. Bennett noticed that the school gymnasium had operating· showers which were no longer in use. She made a trip to the principal's office to gain his permission for using them for Mervin and Grady. He was somewhat surprised that a teacher would bother to take on such a responsibility, but gave his permission.

Next, the aide requested time-off from school to make a Shackleford home visit to discuss the possibility of giving Mervin and Grady showers at school. By this time Miss Cambell was so impressed with the way Mrs. Bennett was handling the situation, that she gladly sent her to the home.

The family lived in an old, white, two-story house which appeared to be well-kept. The inside was unpainted but fairly neat. Mrs. Bennett discovered that the family of twelve resided only on the first floor. This floor was made up of four large rooms, two on each side of the house. They were separated down the middle by a long hallway. The place was quite drafty. At this time of the year it felt good, but would prove to be chilling in the winter months. Fireplaces were the only apparent source of heat.

Mrs. Shackleford welcomed the teacher's aide warmly. The woman was short and heavy set. Mervin looked exactly like her, except for the excess weight. When they entered the kitchen, and Mr. Shackleford stood up, Mrs. Bennett almost "did a double take." This man was an older Grady. He was tall, thin, blonde, and quite good-looking. Three pre-school youngsters were playing on the floor.

It was late for lunch, but the family was getting ready to sit down to a meal of cornbread, turnip greens, and "pot likker." They eagerly invited Mrs. Bennett to join them, but she politely refused on the basis that she had just finished lunch. She did not sit down, for she was afraid of interferring with their meal.

Both parents were receptive to the idea of Mervin and Grady

taking showers at school. In fact, the mother stated how difficult it was "too keep all them young 'uns clean," especially with no running water in the house. They bathed in a tub with water which was hauled from a well, or they used a neighbor's shower once every two or three weeks. Mrs. Shackleford emphasized the fact that she would not be able to provide the boys with clean clothes after the showers, but Mrs. Bennett assured her that it would not be a consideration. They would take care of the clothes at school.

On the way back to school Mrs. Bennett reflected over the problems of Mervin and Grady. The boys came from an impoverished background, were slow academically, had speech difficulties, and were physically weak. She wondered how, if ever, they would be contributing citizens. They seemed to have so many strikes against them.

The relationship between the regular class teacher and the aide was becoming stronger and more positive each day. As the younger woman realized the aide's value, she began to use Mrs. Bennett's services in academic instruction. The aide was bright and quickly learned the techniques of teaching the basic subjects. She even had her own groups of children to work with each day. Since Mrs. Bennett was so interested in Mervin and Grady, they, too, were assigned to her for reading.

Soon after the home visit, the big day of school showers came. Mrs. Bennett had collected two changes of clothes, including socks and underwear, from her own son and neighbors. A hardware store donated a big wash tub. She planned for the boys to learn how to wash their clothes. Mervin and Grady were excited about the event and quickly ran into the shower room. They stayed and stayed and stayed. Finally, after forty minutes they appeared, damp but still smelling badly. When questioned about what they had been doing, it was evident that the boys didn't know how to bathe themselves.

The next day, Mrs. Bennett had one of the younger ministers of the community go in with the boys to assist in the washing process. He returned afterward and told the aide that the boys didn't know how to use soap or the washcloth, much less where their bodies needed concentrated cleaning. On this day they returned smelling good, especially after using deodorant. For the next several months they took showers three times a week.

The plan for having them wash their clothes failed, however. As the weather turned cooler, their hands became chapped and the detergent irritated this condition even more. Mrs. Bennett volunteered to take the dirty clothes home and wash them herself. She also got the boys medicated hand lotion, which they used after showering.

The teachers were amused at the way Marvin and Grady reacted to having underwear. They had never before worn this apparel and had been teased by the other boys many times in their school life. Now, they delighted in showing off their new undergarments. This was accomplished quite subtly by pulling the underpants up high on their waists and stuffing their shirts directly into the underwear rather than over it. Then, they would slide their jeans down over their hips. In this fashion, the whites would show in sufficient portion to raise their esteem among the other fellows.

The boys presented no problems, behaviorially, except that Mervin admired a more aggressive boy in the class and would occasionally follow Jason into mischevious antics. For instance, they began slipping off the school playground and going down to a nearby creek to "catch crawdads." They did this several times before the teachers realized what was happening. The episode was turned into a science project, but the boys were stopped from leaving the school yard.

Since the class was located in a trailer and near the school gymnasium, on rainy days the teachers would let the students run in the gym. This free play in closed quarters led to a good deal of rough-housing. One day Grady fell on the bleacher seats. He bit through his bottom lip and had to be taken to the emergency room for stitches.

Mrs. Bennett knew his mouth would be sore that night; so she went out and got him several cans of soup and straws to take home. When he returned to school the next day he announced how much his mother liked the soup. The entire family had helped him eat it. This was the first time they had ever had canned soup.

Mervin and Grady were improving dramatically in their school work. This was due, in part, to Mrs. Bennett's individualized work, which complemented the resource room teacher's focus. These two teachers worked closely in planning the boys' program, and it obviously had a positive effect.

The other reason which may have contributed to their success was the fact that Miss Cambell and Mrs. Bennett served cereal and milk to several children whom they knew were not eating before coming to school. It was amazing to see how they brightened up with full stomachs.

Toward the end of the year another teacher in the school approached Miss Cambell about letting one of her students take showers with Mervin and Grady. They welcomed the other youngster and sent him in with the older boys. The other teacher, however had failed to receive parental permission. While showering the boy slipped on a piece of soap, fell, and cut his forehead quite badly. Several stitches were needed to repair the wound. Fortunately, the boy's parents weren't concerned and didn't press charges. The principal was frightened enough to cancel all of the bathing at school, however.

The teachers were distressed at this news, but Mervin and Grady had been "bitten" by the cleanliness bug. Their older sister told Mrs. Bennett that the boys were using the neighbor's shower frequently. She quoted them as saying they itched when they didn't bathe.

As the last few days of the year arrived, Mervin and Grady began talking about how much they didn't want school to be out for the summer. Mrs. Bennett finally questioned them about their reasons, and Grady said "Mi' Benny, we gotta wok in the 'bacca feel wid Daddy, and we gets so hongry." A strained look came over his face as he doubled his fist and put it to his stomach. "My belly huts so bad." Mrs. Bennett answered with, "I know its hard Grady, but we just have to keep going. I'll be here next year to help you." The aide was being moved up to the sixth grade room, where the boys had been assigned for the next year.

Mrs. Bennett returned to night school at the local college that next year and within two years, she had completed a degree in special education. She became a resource room teacher for educable mentally retarded youngsters in that community.

Stimulus Question

1. In what ways may a teacher's aide be of service in the classroom? Should the lead teacher have input into the selection of an aide? Why?

2. How often do children usually receive speech therapy? Do you believe Mervin and Grady will profit from this? Why?

3. What were some of the characteristics of Mervin and Grady that initially worried Mrs. Bennett?

4. What types of classes should be placed in trailers and in supplementary buildings when the main school building will no longer accommodate all of the classes?

5. Is it proper for teachers to try to gain information about children from sources other than school records? What are the possible benefits from doing so?

6. What alternatives, other than showers at school, do teachers have when there is an odor problem with some of the students?

7. Whose responsibility is it to make home visits, the aide or the teacher?

8. Would you consider the home visit made by Mrs. Bennett a success? Why?

9. The negative aspects of Mervin and Grady's situation were mentioned. What are the positive things they had going for them?

10. Who else besides the minister could the teachers have used to assist the boys with their showers?

11. Do you think Mrs. Bennett was overly involved with Mervin and Grady? Why?

12. How could the teachers have avoided the gym accident?

13. Give ways in which Mrs. Bennett made a difference in Mervin and Grady's lives.

14. What do you consider to be the hidden curriculum?

THE MIGRANTS

The single complex school was located in a rural area in the midwest. It had fifteen classrooms, two gymnasiums, a lunchroom, and an outdoor pool. The staff consisted of thirteen regular class teachers, two special class teachers, a part-time reading specialist, and a high school principal.

The school was run by the iron-clad hold of a tall, sixty-year-old superintendent who looked more like a movie star cowboy than the typical educator. He had been at the school for years, knew legislators around the state, and could write grant proposals, which almost always got funded.

The superintendent made unbelievable use of his faculty. The high school principal was the basketball coach, and he taught high school science. One of the special education teachers was the wrestling coach. The sixth grade homeroom and math teacher was the elementary school principal and elementary physical education teacher. Each teacher had at least two different jobs. The most outstanding program however, was the free or inexpensive breakfast prepared by the lunchroom staff. All teachers and students were allowed to participate, and no one went into the classroom hungry.

Manuel attended this school. He was an eight-year-old child from a Mexican-American family. He was a happy, cheerful boy who always had a wave and a smile for everyone. He made friends easily and was well-liked by the other children. His best friend, Pedro, was also eight years old. He was a member of the only other Chicano family in the school.

Manuel's family consisted of the parents and eight children, who ranged in age from two through sixteen. They lived in a trailer, which they pulled with them in their search for farm work. They had lived in this community for the past five months.

Manuel's family spoke only Spanish at home, and because of this, the children were having difficulties in reading English. Manuel was no exception. He received extra help from Mr. Martin, the part-time reading specialist. Manuel was only reading on a first grade level; thus, his second grade teacher had reservations about promoting him to the third grade.

Since Mr. Martin planned to teach remedial reading in the summer school program, it was thought that the boy could profit from this extra instruction. In addition to the tutoring, Manuel would have free use of the pool and wrestling instruction. Rather than merely sending a note home, Mr. Martin volunteered to make a home visit to discuss the summer program thoroughly with Manuel's parents. The teacher could understand Spanish and speak it on a limited basis.

Mr. Martin went to visit the home on his lunch hour. This was convenient, for the trailer was parked on a corner lot about two blocks from the school. There was little or no yard, only a small dirt driveway. The trailer had once been painted aqua, but now it was faded and peeling in many places. Old wooden steps led up to the trailer's door. Mr. Martin knocked, and Manuel's mother came to the door. She smiled warmly and motioned for him to enter.

Even though the western sun was shining brightly, the inside of the trailer was dark with only one light hanging from a cord in the kitchen area. There was one small high window between the kitchen and living area, allowing very little natural light. The living area was filled with large, worn, over-stuffed chairs and one long sofa. On one table was a small television set with rabbit ears off to one side. Although cluttered, the rooms were clean. There seemed to Mr. Martin to be three other small rooms to the left of the living area and, obviously, only one bathroom.

Manuel's mother spoke in Spanish. She conveyed the information to Mr. Martin that her husband was out working on a farm, and she, too, should be there. She had been ill that morning, and her husband insisted that she stay home. The three preschoolers were out back playing with neighbor children. When she worked, these younger children went with them. A sitter was a luxury they could not afford.

The woman, herself, was quite large. Her dark hair was straight and cut neck-length. The sides were pulled back from her face and held up over her ears with bobbie pins. She also had bangs, which had been unevenly cut. Her age could have been anywhere from thirty to forty-five. The years of hard farm work had taken their toll on her appearance.

Mr. Martin explained about the summer school program. The woman was quite agreeable for Manuel and two of her other children to participate.

That summer proved to be beneficial for Manuel in several ways. His reading and spoken English improved so dramatically that by August he was approaching reading at grade level. He learned to swim in the school pool and looked forward to that with eagerness each day. He wasn't excited about the wrestling, but he did go along with the program.

The family was able to continue working in the area until the middle of September, and then they were gone. No one at the school knew where they intended to move. Nothing was heard from the family that winter.

The following April the family returned but their situation had changed. Manuel's father appeared at school looking sad and defeated. He related their story to the superintendent.

After leaving, the family moved into a barrio that was located on the outskirts of a large city. Manuel's father hoped to find work here during the winter months. In November, one-hundred-mile-an-hour winds flipped over the unanchored trailer. The flames from the gas heater engulfed the trailer and turned it into a virtual inferno. That eventful day, Manuel had been left at home alone with the three younger children while his older brothers and sisters were helping his parents look for work. The little ones died in the fire, but a neighbor managed to save Manuel. The boy was badly burned.

Fortunately, their location was near a nationally known burn center, so Manuel was taken there immediately. The burns extended over the upper portion of his body. Both hands were burned, and he had lost most of his fingers on his right hand. His neck and face were also involved, and his left ear had to be removed.

Manuel's mother fell into such emotional shambles, that she

could not bear to visit Manuel after seeing him once. Two weeks after the accident, she left the family. They had no idea where or with whom she went.

Meanwhile, the family's plight had received top news notice and soon food, clothing, housewares, etc., began pouring in to them. The most valuable gift, however, was a used trailer. This trailer was considerably more durable and larger than the previous one. The father was determined to keep the family together. He and the four oldest children moved into their new home. He found janitorial work near the hospital; thus he was able to visit Manuel each day.

Manuel experienced four painful operations between November and April. Finally, he was released and allowed to go home. After returning to the trailer, Manuel announced that he wanted to return to the community where Mr. Martin and Pedro lived. Since his father had been worried that the authorities would soon ask to see his immigration card, the family left the barrio and was traveling northward within three days.

The superintendent relayed the family's story to his faculty. The school personnel were saddened to hear of the family's troubles. They were shocked to see little Manuel with such disfigurement on his face and hands. He was no longer the attractive child they had known several months before. Scabs were prominent where his ear had been. There were also huge, red scars on his neck and face. His stubby right hand hung limply at his side. Only his large, brown eyes remained the same.

Although Manuel had been out of school almost six months, the superintendent thought it would be best if the youngster were placed in the third grade with his old friends. Since there had been no time to prepare the children for Manuel's appearance at school the first day, they all stared at him. His old friend, Pedro was no exception. By lunch time, a few were even teasing him. The superintendent quickly put an end to this treatment by paddling those that participated in the teasing.

In spite of the fact that the teasing was under control, Manuel was still having a difficult time. The other children were simply unwilling to interact with the child. Even Pedro would have nothing to do with him. They were either repulsed or afraid of him. Since this was the first school he had attended since the accident, he stopped trying to play, and he began going off by himself at recess time. After school he played with his other siblings. They seemed to have no difficulty accepting him. He was still just Manuel to them. In the classroom he sat off to the side and responded only when he was spoken to or when a question was directed at him. His teacher simply did not know how to cope with him. Actually, she, too, was repulsed at Manuel's disfigurement. His withdrawal made it easier for her not to deal with her own feelings.

Manuel's only respite from the long hours in the classroom was his contact with Mr. Martin. Since Manuel had missed so much academic work, he was assigned to Mr. Martin for an hour each day. This setting proved to be his haven. Here, he was accepted. Mr. Martin had not changed his attitude toward him, and so their relationship continued to flourish. Manuel also found that the children who were seeing Mr. Martin during his period were also more accepting of him than those children who were in the regular class.

Manuel's father had been able to find farm work in the area; so they hoped to be able to stay until Manuel had to return to the hospital for more corrective surgery. The father was determined to keep his children together. There was still no word from the mother.

Stimulus Question

1. The school was described as being well-equipped. How would you describe the atmosphere?
2. Do you believe teachers are effective when being responsible for several jobs?
3. How do you believe Manuel's family was treated in the community, since the family was transient?
4. Is not reading at grade level enough criteria for not promoting a child? What else should influence the decision?
5. Should child care be provided for young children of working mothers?
6. What is a barrio?
7. What help should have been provided for Manuel's mother after the accident? What help should Manuel have received?

8. What is an immigration card? Why was Manuel's father worried about his?
9. Do you think the superintendent made a wise decision about Manuel's teasing? What else could he have done?
11. What could the school personnel have done about the way the children treated Manuel?
12. Who should have helped the teacher with her feelings? It is unusual for one to react in such a way to a physical disfigurement? Why?
13. Why were the special education children more accepting?
14. Should someone have helped the family find Manuel's mother? Who?
15. What do you suppose will happen to Manuel? Do you believe the other school children will ever come to accept Manuel?
16. How can cultural differences affect the performance of students in the classroom?
17. Does Public Law 94-142 apply to children of non-English linguistic backgrounds? Explain.

THE JUNK MAN'S SON

The rural town of Madisonville contained a population of approximately 3,000 people. Madisonville Elementary School was located on a street directly behind the business district, and, although it was the smallest school in the county, it was the center of social activity for the community. The town's residents strongly supported all of the school's sporting events, and the clubs held their meetings in the cafeteria.

It was a crisp, clear morning in November when Willis Messer and his father appeared at the principal's office to enroll Willis in the school. Although they had no school record in hand, Mr. Messer described Willis' school history. The ten-year-old boy had attended residential school for emotionally disturbed children for several years. Mr. Messer then explained that last year he removed Willis, because he could receive forty-eight dollars a month from the government for child care if the boy was with him at home. The father was having difficulty living off his welfare check.

Willis had been attending school since September in a larger community several miles away, but he had been so disruptive that Mr. Messer decided to move and give Willis a chance at a new school. The principal loved a challenge and in spite of this history promised the father that, one way or another, they would keep Willis in school.

Mr. Messer and Willis moved into a run-down house within a block of the school. The father soon became known as the "junk man." He spent his days going through the local garbage dump and hauling what he considered to be salvageable items back to the house. It wasn't long before the house and yard looked similar to the dump.

135

The teachers at the school were curious about Willis's background. It was quickly discovered that Willis was the only offspring of poverty-stricken, aging parents. Three years after his birth, Mrs. Messer abandoned Willis and his father. The child spent the remainder of his preschool years with an aunt. When Willis entered school, he went to live with his father.

Willis first entered Madisonville Elementary School dressed fairly decently, although his wardrobe consisted of only one pair of jeans, a shirt, and tennis shoes. He had an old winter coat, which was several sizes too large. This set of clothes was never washed, so it wasn't long before they were discarded. Willis began wearing his father's old pants, which he had cut off at the legs to legs to fit, and although they were quite baggy, he managed to hold them up with a rope tied to his waist. He wore an over-sized, ripped shirt that had several buttons missing. When the tennis shoes wore out, he replaced them with a scuffed-up pair of man's boots which he had found at the dump. He "clumped" around in these and never wore socks or shoe laces. He held the boots together by tying a string around the top portion of the boots.

Physically, Willis was average height and on the stocky side. He had light blue eyes, a smooth, creamy complexion, and light blonde hair. The few times he washed himself, his yellow hair added to his attractiveness. The boy bathed so seldom, however, that his body odor was offensive.

Willis was placed in the only fifth grade class in the school. There were no supportive services for emotionally handicapped children. The child had to cope alone. He was hyperactive and aggressive, and had an explosive temper along with an abusive vocabulary.

The teachers weren't certain about his level of academic functioning, so they provided him with third grade materials. This did no good. Willis did not work, and he used every excuse to get out of his assigned seat to wander aimlessly about the room. His one asset was his verbal ability. It approached giftedness. He could carry on an interesting, intelligent conversation with the teachers, but at the same time he stubbornly refused to carry out the assignments and argued endlessly about them, usually in a loud, booming tone. When it was apparent to Willis that he was losing an argument, he would have a temper tantrum.

Willis's homeroom teacher avoided arguments with him, and as long as he wasn't disturbing anyone left him alone. She tried to be kind and understanding. The math teacher, Mr. Rob approached the matter differently. He was a young teacher, just two years out of college. In spite of the fact that he coached junior high teams, he was still on the pudgy side, especially in his face and stomach. His method of teaching math was to scream problems at the children in hopes that an answer would be forthcoming. If no one responded correctly, he would throw books into the aisles or slam them on the desk.

When a youngster could not answer a question correctly, did not complete homework on time, rocked back on two legs of a chair, or chewed gum, "Big Red," an enormous, thick, red paddle, was brought forth. The guilty child was taken outside the room and a long discussion would ensue between him and Mr. Rob. These discussions went on sometimes as long as thirty minutes with the child frantically trying to talk his way out of the paddling. In no instance were they successful, for Mr. Rob always administered five licks to the backside of the students.

This punishment was a daily occurance at Madisonville Elementary School. Parents often complained, for their children, both boys and girls, were coming home with broken blood vessels and black and blue marks on their behinds. In addition, many of the children were tearful at the thought of attending this math class. The complaints were to no avail, for the prinicipal stood behind his teachers and was strongly in favor of corporal punishment.

Willis was beaten more than any other fifth grader. Without fail, he would get into an argument with Mr. Rob and would be hauled out of the class for his licks. Before the paddling was over, Willis would be screaming in pain, and he actually tried to climb the cement block walls of the hall to get away from his attacker. The principal approved of the punishment, for the school was demonstrating that it could control Willis enough to keep him in line and in school. For a day or two, Willis would cooperate then he would start causing disruption again.

Another problem area for Willis was his relationship with the other children. They made fun of his large, old clothes and body odor and wouldn't allow him to join in with their games. He was especially teased during physical education, for he couldn't manuever himself well in large boots. The boy had no friends, and, when he wasn't arguing, he spent his free time walking around the school yard watching the other children play. He often got into fights on the playground and was paddled frequently for this.

The boy's treatment at home was no better than what he received at school. Neighbors complained about Willis's screaming during the night. Mr. Messer drank heavily and would take out his aggression on Willis. He beat the boy with a stick, an automobile fan belt, or anything else he could conveniently find. The paddlings at school were often administered on top of large welts and bruises he received at home. Indeed, his behavior at school often reflected his home treatment.

Willis never took any money to school for lunch. Instead, he walked home at noon for the meal. On one occasion, he became sick in the afternoon with stomach cramps and reported to a teacher that he had eaten meat which had been sitting out on the table for three days. His father refused to sign the papers for Willis to receive a free lunch at school. There was nothing the school personnel could do but to continue letting the boy go home to eat.

Although the school had no program for emotionally handicapped students, they did have a part-time reading teacher, who had been hired on Title I funds. This teacher, Mrs. Harrison, began teaching in January, and Willis was immediately assigned to her. She came to the school three days a week. For an hour each of these days, Willis received individual tutoring in reading.

An informal reading assessment showed that Willis was reading at the second preprimer level. His comprehension abilities far surpassed this, but his word recognition skills were extremely weak. He had only a few sight words in his reading vocabulary. This assessment was difficult to ascertain, for Willis was uncooperative. He did not want to leave the classroom to attend the sessions and would linger back as long as possible. When he did enter the physical setting of the lesson, he wouldn't discuss topics or read out of a book.

In desperation, Mrs. Harrison went to a large reading center and rented a reading series that included a machine that played records and, at the same time, showed film strips to accompany the stories on the records. In this manner, Willis could listen to and view stories that were interesting to him without having to read the words. Comprehension questions were asked after each story, and Willis always achieved perfection in this.

After a few sessions with the special machine, Willis came to the reading lesson without hesitation. Mrs. Harrison slowly began introducing words to Willis by a multisensory approach. She would ask him which words in the story he would like to learn, and these were taught one at a time. Unfortunately, Willis' emotional problem prevented much success. Often, he would enter the reading situation distraught because of a "run in" with other students or Mr. Rob. He would either pace around the room or face the wall and pick at it with his fingers. No amount of talk or bribery would settle him down to work.

After a couple of months had elapsed, Willis announced that he wanted to write a story. Delighted, Mrs. Harrison agreed to write the story, while the boy dictated it. His imagination was astounding. The story was well thought out, occurred in logical order, and his vocabulary was highly developed. Mrs. Harrison took it home and typed it for him. Then she suggested he work on learning words in the story. This technique proved successful, and for the remainder of the year Willis and Mrs. Harrison worked in this manner. At the end of the year, Willis brought all of his typed stories to Mrs. Harrison, and they bound them in one volume called, "Stories by Willis Messer."

The following fall Willis's father decided the boy was costing him more money at home than he was receiving from the government for keeping him. He took Willis back to the residential school where he still remains.

Stimulus Questions

1. What kinds of assessment should the teachers have given Willis to determine his abilities?
2. Even though he could argue well, should the teachers have entered into debates with Willis? Why?
3. Is paddling the way to cope with a disturbed child? Why? What are other techniques that could have been used more effectively?

4. If the parents objected to corporal punishment in the schools, why do you think it continued? What other routes are open to parents to prevent such action by the schools?
5. What was more important to the principal, his school record or his students?
6. What should his teachers have done to help Willis with his relationships with other children?
7. Should the neighbors have reported the child abuse to social agencies? What is this procedure?
8. How could the school handle the situation about the free lunch and get Willis the food he needed?
9. Why did Willis refuse to read the words, but do so well when dictated to Mrs. Harrison?
10. Why was Willis able to learn to read the words of the stories he dictated to Mrs. Harrison?
11. What other methods of teaching reading could Mrs. Harrison have tried with Willis?

THE CYCLE OF POVERTY

The self-contained special education class for trainable mentally retarded children was made up of eight youngsters who ranged in chronological age from five to ten. Six-year-old Grace Ledbetter was a member of this class. She was small in stature; she had short, straight, red hair; and her face was covered with freckles. Her baby teeth had not yet fallen out, and these were in deperate need of dental work. When she smiled, one could see her decayed teeth.

Grace was functioning on a mental level above most of the children in the class, however, she was not able to participate in a normal kindergarten or first grade setting. Socially, emotionally, physically, and intellectually, her development was more typical of a three-year-old child. She was toilet trained, was beginning to learn to dress herself, and could feed herself with her fingers. Grace's speech and language skills were extremely underdeveloped. Her vocabulary consisted of one and two words, for example, "Me cookie," "Me pee-pee," "Want juice." Even these words were difficult to understand, for the child had many distortions and substitutions of the speech sounds.

Her attention span was short, and she was hyperactive. She would literally bounce from one activity to another all during the day. Also, her behavior was quite demanding. If her wants were not immediately satisfied, she would fly into a temper tantrum.

Her favorite activity was listening to stories being read orally by one of the teachers. Each morning her first act was to gather up an armload of books and approach the teacher with "Weed me." Since this had a calming effect on her, and she was so demanding it was hard to refuse her. Reading stories aloud to the children who would listen was a frequent daily occurence in the class.

Another factor complicating Grace's education was her home life. Her mother, Liz, had grown up with her grandparents in an economically deprived home. Liz's parents had abandoned her at an early age, and her maternal grandparents had reluctantly taken her in to live with them. They had five of their own children living with them at the time. It was an added strain for them to accept Liz.

As a child, Liz was not attractive, was slow in school, and was ignored both at school by the teachers and at home by her grandparents. Starving for attention and affection, Liz began having sexual relations at the age of twelve. On many occasions, she would copulate with as many as ten boys at a time. It is likely that she escaped veneral disease, because the boys were young, and for many, Liz was their first encounter with sex. She used no birth control and, three years later, at the age of fifteen, she became pregnant with Grace.

When Liz's grandparents realized she was pregnant, her grandfather beat her severely with a thick board. As Liz was attempting to escape from his brutal beating, she fell down several stairs and was knocked unconscious for two days. This incident frightened the grandfather enough to allow Liz to remain with them until after Grace's birth. The grandparents shortly began to exert pressure on her to move out of their house. A year later, Liz began seeing Tom, and when she became pregnant again, they decided to get married.

Tom Ledbetter was a twenty-two-year-old unemployed man who listed "mechanic" as his occupation. In reality, however, his training and experience had been limited to pumping gas at a local service station for three months when he was eighteen. He did tinker occasionally with old cars, but his primary source of income was through welfare. He had dropped out of school at age sixteen and wandered aimlessly about the country until he met Liz. He had no connection with his own family and had a jail record for drinking and brawling in bars and taverns.

After Liz and Tom were married, they moved into a two-room shack, which they had converted from a large, abandoned chicken coop. The residence contained a dirt floor and had no electricity or running water. They carried water from a neighbor's well almost a quarter of a mile away. Plastic was taped over the cracks in the wall, and a warped door was leaning against the front entrance. For heat they used an old wood stove that Tom had found in the local dump. Whenever he collected enough wood, they had a fire. Their toilet was a hole Tom had dug in a wooded area near the house. He stretched two logs across it for a seat.

Four months after they were married, Liz delivered a baby boy. A month after this child was born, she became pregnant once again. This time, she had another girl. Tom spent his days drinking, loafing around the house, and having sex with Liz. The babies crawled and toddled around the dirt floor. The babies were fed saltine crackers and powdered milk while Tom, Liz, and Grace ate cold, canned goods, such as spaghetti, ravioli, corn, and potatoes.

Liz made somewhat of an effort to clean the children, but with poor toilet facilities, lack of running water, and the dirt floor, it was difficult to accomplish. The babies wore the same diaper for days at a time, and thus both were blistered with diaper rash. They were beyond the screaming state, but whined their way through the day in hopes they would be given food. In addition, they were covered with scaly, peeling skin.

About the same time Grace started school, Liz became pregnant again. Realizing that they did not have enough food for the five of them, she attempted a self-induced abortion. She was effective in using a coat hanger to bring on the abortion, but the bleeding was so profuse that a panicked Tom borrowed a neighbor's car and took her to the emergency room. The doctor saved Liz, but in the process had to do a complete hysterectomy.

Grace appeared at school each day filthy and smelling of excrement. Her skin was crusty and peeling in many places. It wasn't long before the teacher discovered lice in her head. The school nurse verified the situation and contacted the local health department. At the same time, a note was sent home to Liz about the infestation. Before the health department could intervene, Liz had shaved Grace's head. The child appeared at school the next day totally bald.

Because of her skin condition, the teachers were fearful that Grace may be a source of contagion for the other youngsters, so they began to give her a daily bath in a large sink that happened to be in the room.

Through donations, they were able to collect several changes of the proper size clothing. For a few days, Grace kept returning to school wearing her old soiled clothes. When the child was asked what happened to the new clothes, she responded with, "Tom taked." From then on, the child wore her new clothes only at school. Before school was out each day, she changed back into her old clothes. At least the teachers were able to keep her in clean outfits.

As far as her physical condition was concerned, Grace's hair soon began to grow out, and by washing her hair frequently at school, they were able to prevent another battle with lice. The school nurse was treating her scaling skin with some degree of success. Grace was apparently coming to school without having eaten; so the teachers took it upon themselves to provide her with cereal and milk each morning. Even so, when her lunch tray was brought in, the child became so excited over the food, that she had to be restrained from attacking the person carrying the tray. She gobbled up her food quickly and would eat any left-overs from the other children's trays.

One Monday morning Grace appeared at school acting strangely. She was unusually quiet and walked slowly with rigid, stiff movements. The youngster withdrew into a corner where she sat on the floor and hugged her knees. When the teacher approached her to give her a bath, she began to scream. The screaming grew louder and louder until she was totally hysterical. Not being able to calm her, they called the principal. He came in, lifted up the child, and took her screaming into his office. He offered her some cookies, and she quieted enough to stuff them into her mouth. When the cookies had been eaten, she responded with "Mo. Mo." Seeing that she was settled, he walked her back to the classroom.

The morning progressed with no other outburst. After the children's naps, the teacher decided to take a chance and try to bathe her again. She was dirty from not having been cleaned over the weekend. This attempt proved to be successful, but as they pulled off her clothes, Grace flinched with pain. It was then that they noticed her entire right side and thigh was badly bruised. Grace often had bruises, but nothing severe. When asked what had caused them, Grace answered, "Tom do." One teacher asked, "How did Tom do it?" Grace responded with, "Big car." The teacher was puzzled, because they knew the family did not have a car.

The school nurse was called in to examine the child, and she realized the necessity of having a physician see her. She took Grace to the hospital where they were met by social service workers whom the principal had called. Upon finishing the examination, the physician declared that Grace had three broken ribs, but was otherwise not seriously hurt.

Grace was taken from the hospital to a temporary foster home. The social workers went directly to see Liz and Tom. When they arrived, Liz was gone, and Tom was lying drunk in front of the house. The babies were unattended in the house. They were filthy and obviously had not eaten in a couple of days. Tom was arrested for possible child abuse and neglect, and a warrant was sent out for Liz's arrest. The babies were taken to the same foster home as Grace.

The next day Liz voluntarily appeared at the county jail. She was in hysterics wanting to know the whereabouts of her children. She explained to the police that her grandfather had died, and she had gone home to attend the funeral, leaving the children in Tom's care. The police told her the story of Grace's physical condition and that all the children were in a foster home. By this time the officers had gotten the story of Grace's condition from Tom. It seems that he had borrowed a neighbor's car to "go to the store," and while backing out of the driveway, he had hit the child. He stated that he thought she wasn't hurt and saw no need in seeking medical attention. He was to be held in custody until a judge could hear the case. Liz was released and referred to social services.

Here, she was told that in order to get the children back she must move to a more suitable location and demonstrate that she was responsible enough to take care of the children. She was assigned a social worker to assist her in these tasks. Several months later, when Tom had been released on probation, they were allowed to move into a low-income housing complex. Liz and Tom both wanted the children back in their custody, so Tom found a job working as a custodian at a local factory. His income was meager, but with welfare assistance, social services felt that the situation was vastly improved. The children were returned to their parents with hopes that the family could remain together.

Stimulus Questions

1. How did Grace's mother's background influence the child?
2. How do you think the teachers reacted to Grace's demands that she be read to much of the day? Do you see an underlying need by this behavior?
3. Could the welfare department have done anything to improve the Ledbetter's living conditions?
4. Why do you suppose the medical people didn't intervene when Liz was brought in with the self-induced abortion? Where could she have gone for help before the abortion? Was she right in not wanting to have another child?
5. Was it the teacher's responsibility to bathe Grace each day? Explain.
6. What should the teachers have done about Tom's taking the clean clothes from Grace?
7. Should the teachers have called in the principal to settle down the hysterical child? What else could have been done?
8. Who do you suppose placed Grace in a foster home? Was this a good decision? Why?
9. Did the court have a legal case against Tom?
10. Should the children have been given back to Tom and Liz?
11. What do you think the family's chances of making it are? What kind of support would they need?
12. What is the cycle of poverty?

SUGGESTED READINGS

Axline, Virginia, M.: *Dibs in Search of Self.* New York, Random House, 1964.

Bach, Richard: *Jonathan Livingston Seagull.* New York, Macmillan, 1970.

Bereiter, Carl and Ennglemann, Seigfried: *Teaching Disadvantaged Children in the Preschool.* Englewood-Cliffs, Prentice-Hall, 1966.

Berman, Louise: *New Priorities in the Curriculum.* Columbus, Charles E. Merrill, 1967.

Berne, Eric: *Games People Play.* New York, Grove Press, 1964.

Black, W.: Self concept as related to achievement and age in learning disabled children. *Child Development, 45:*1137-1140, 1974.

Bridgers, Sue Ellen: *All Together Now.* New York, Kopf, 1979.

Bruner, Jerome: *On Knowing.* Cambridge, Balknap Press, 1964.

Buck, Pearl S.: *The Child Who Never Grew.* New York, John Day, 1950.

Canfield, Jack and Wells, Harold C.: *100 Ways to Enhance Self Concept in the Classroom: A Handbook for Teachers and Parents.* Englewood Cliffs, Prentice Hall, 1976.

Casteel, J. and Stahl, R.: *Value Clarification in the Classroom: A Primer.* Pacific Palisades, Goodyear, 1975.

Castillo, Gloria A.: *Left-Handed Teaching.* New York, Holt, Reinhart, and Winston, 1978.

Carter, Thomas P.: The negative self concept of Mexican-American students. *School and Society, 96:*217-219, 1968.

Combs, Arthur W. (Ed.): *Perceiving, Behaving, Becoming.* Washington, Yearbook of the Association for Supervision and Curriculum Development, 1962.

Combs, Arthur W., Avila, Donald L., and Purkey, W.W.: *The Helping Relationships: Basic Concepts for the Helping Professions.* Boston, Allyn and Bacon, 1971.

Conroy, Pat: *The Water is Wide.* Boston, Houghton-Mifflin, 1972.

Craig, Elenor: *P.S. Your Not Listening.* New York, R.W. Baron, 1972.

Cullum, A.: *The Geranium on the Window Sill Just Died But Teacher You Went Right On.* Holland, Hartin Quist.

Dennison, George: *The Lives of Children.* New York, Random House, 1969.

Derlega, V.J. and Chaikin, A.L.: *Sharing Intimacy: What We Reveal to Others and Why.* Englewood Cliffs, Prentice-Hall, 1975.

Deutsch, Martin: The disadvantaged child and the learning process. In Passow, A. Harry (Ed.): *Education in Depressed Areas.* New York, Columbia University, 1963.

Dinkmeyer, Don C.: *Child Development: The Emerging Self.* Englewood Cliffs, Prentice-Hall, 1965.

Dollar, Barry: *Humanizing Classroom Discipline: A Behavioral Approach,* New York, Harper and Row, 1972.

Dobson, Russell and Dobson, Judith Shelton: *Humaneness in Schools: A Neglected Force,* Debuque, Kendall/Hunt, 1976.

Dreikurs, Rudolf, Grunwald, Bernice, and Pepper, Floy: *Maintaining Sanity in the Classroom.* New York, Harper and Row, 1971.

Dreikurs, Rudolf and Cassel, P.: *Discipline Without Tears.* New York, Hawthorne, 1974.

Eareckson, Joni: *Joni.* Minneapolis, World Wide, 1976.

Exupéry, Antonine de Saint: *The Little Prince.* New York, Harcourt, Brace and World, 1943.

Fantini, Mario and Weinstein, Gerald: *The Disadvantaged.* New York, Harper and Row, 1968.

Felker, E.W.: *Building Positive Self-Concepts.* Minneapolis, Burgess, 1974.

Fromm, Erick: *The Art of Loving.* New York, Harper and Row, 1963.

Ganzda, George M., Asbury, Frank R., Balzer, Fred J., Childers, William C., and Walters, Richard P.: *Human Relations De-*

velopment: A Manual for Educators. Boston, Allyn and Bacon, 1973.

Ginott, Jaim: *Teacher and Child.* New York, Macmillan, 1972.

Glasser, William: *Reality Therapy.* New York, Harper and Row, 1965.

Glasser, William: *Schools without Failure.* New York, Harper and Row, 1969.

Greenberg, Joanne: *In This Sign.* New York, Holt, Rinehart and Winston, 1970.

Gregory, Dick and Lipstye, Robert: *Nigger.* New York, Simon and Schuster, 1964.

Griffin, John Howard: *Black Like Me.* Boston, Houghton Mifflin, 1977.

Griffin, John Howard: *A Time to be Human.* New York, Macmillan, 1977.

Gross, Beatrice: *Radical School Reform.* New York, Simon and Schuster, 1969.

Harris, Thomas Anthony: *I'm OK; You're OK.* New York, Harper and Row, 1970.

Hendon, James: *The Way It Spozed to Be.* New York, Simon and Schuster, 1969.

Hinde, Robert A. (Ed.): *Non-Verbal Communication.* New York, Cambridge University Press, 1972.

Huxley, Aldous: *Brave New World.* New York, Harper and Row, 1947.

Insel, P. and Jacobson, L.: *What do You Expect? An Inquiry Into Self-Fulfilling Prophecies.* Menlo Park, Cummings, 1975.

Jones, Richard Matthew: *Fantasy and Feeling in Education.* New York, University Press, 1968.

Kelley, Earl Clarence: *Humanizing the Education of Children.* Washington, National Education Association, 1969.

Keller, Helen: *The Story of My Life.* New York, Doubleday, 1954.

Keys, Daniel: *Flowers for Algernon.* New York, Harcourt, Brace, and Jovanovich, 1966.

Kohl, Herbert: *36 Children.* New York, The New American Library, 1968.

Kozol, Jonathan: *Death At An Early Age.* New York, Bantam Books, 1968.

Landry, R.G. and Edeburn, C.E.: *Teacher Self-Concept and*

Student Self-Concept. Paper presented at American Educational Research Association Convention, Chicago, 1974.

Layden, Milton: *Escaping the Hostility Trap.* Englewood Cliffs, Prentice-Hall, 1977.

Lee, Harper: *To Kill a Mockingbird.* New York, J.B. Lippincott, 1960.

Leonard, George Burr: *Education and Ecstacy.* New York, Delcorte Press, 1968.

Little, Jean: *Mine for Keeps.* Boston, Little, Brown, 1962.

MacCracken, Mary: *A Circle of Children.* Philadelphia, Lippincott, 1974.

Maslow, Abraham: *Motivation and Personality.* New York, Harper and Row, 1954.

Maslow, Abraham Harold: Personality problems and personality growth. In Moustakas, Clark E. (Ed.): *The Self: Explorations in Personal Growth.* New York, Harper, 1956.

Master, Edgar Lee: *Spoon River Anthology.* New York, Macmillan, 1948.

May, Rollo: *Man's Search for Himself.* New York, Norton, 1953.

May, Rollo: *Love and Will.* New York, Norton, 1969.

Melton, David: *A Boy Called Hopeless.* New York, Scholastic Book Services, 1977.

Montagu, Ashley: *On Being Human.* New York, Hawthorne Books. 1967.

Montagu, Ashley: *The Elephant Man.* New York, E.P. Dutton, 1971.

Moody, Ann: *Coming of Age in Mississippi.* New York, Dial Press, 1968.

Moustakas, Clark E.: *The Authentic Teacher: Sensitivity and Awareness in the Classroom.* Cambridge, Howard A. Doyle, 1966.

Neill, Alexander Sutherland: *Summerhill.* New York, Hart, 1960.

Neufeld, John: *Lisa, Bright and Dark.* New York, Signet, 1969.

Newman, Mildred and Berkowitz, Bernard: *How To Be Your Own Best Friend.* New York, Random House, 1973.

Paulas, Trina: *Hope for the Flowers.* New York, Paulist Press, 1972.

Powell, John: *Why Am I Afraid to Tell You Who I Am?* Chicago,

Argus Communication, 1969.

Purkey, William Watson: *Self Concept and School Achievement.* Englewood Cliffs, Prentice-Hall, 1970.

Purkey, William Watson: *Inviting School Success.* Belmont, Wadsworth, 1978.

Raths, Louis, Harmin, Merrill, and Simon, Sidney: *Values and Teaching: Working with Values in the Classroom.* Columbus Charles E. Merrill, 1966.

Reis, R.: Learning your students' names. *Education,* 93:45-46, 1972.

Reisman, Frank: *The Culturally Deprived Child.* New York, Harper and Row, 1962.

Reich, Charles: *The Greening of America.* New York, Random House, 1970.

Robert, Marc: *Loneliness in the Schools.* Niles, Argus Communications, 1974.

Rogers, Carl Ranson: *Client-Centered Therapy.* Boston, Houghton Mifflin, 1951.

Rogers, Carl Ransom: *Coming Into Existence.* New York, World Publishing, 1967.

Rogers, Carl Ransom: *Freedom to Learn.* Columbus, Charles E. Merrill, 1969.

Rogers, Dale Evans: *Angel Unaware.* Westwood, Elming H. Revell, 1954.

Rosenthal, Robert and Jacobson, Leonore: *Pygmalion in the Classroom.* New York, Holt, Rinehart, and Winston, 1968.

Rubin, Louis, J.: *Facts and Feelings in the Classroom.* New York, Viking Press, 1973.

Scobey, Mary-Margaret, and Graham, Grace (Eds.): *To Nurture Humaneness.* Washington, Yearbook of the Association for Supervision and Curriculum Development, 1970.

Silberman, Charles E.: *Crisis in the Classroom.* New York, Random House, 1970.

Simon, Sidney B.: *Negative Criticism.* Niles, Argus Communications, 1978.

Simon, Sidney, Howe, Leland, and Kirschenbaum, Howard: *Values Clarification: A Handbook of Practical Strategies for Teachers and Students.* New York, Hart, 1972.

Toffler, Alvin: *Future Shock*. New York, Bantam Books, 1971.

Valett, Robert E.: *Humanistic Education: Developing the Total Person*. Saint Louis, C.V. Mosby, 1977.

Warden, Sarah: *The Left-Outs*. New York, Holt, Rinehart and Winston, 1968.

Weinstein, Gerald and Fantini, Mario (Eds.): *Toward Humanistic Education: A Curriculum of Affect*. New York, Prager Publishers, 1970.

Williams, Margery: *The Velveteen Rabbit*. New York, Avon Books, 1975.

Young, Leontine: *Wednesday's Children: A Study of Child Neglect and Abuse*. New York, McGraw-Hill, 1971.

INDEX

153